SUPERKID ACADEMY

A SIMPLE GUIDE FOR HOME USE

THE HEART OF A SUPERKID

BIBLE STUDY FOR KIDS!

Ordinary kids doing extraordinary things through the power of God's Word!

Superkid Academy Home Bible Study for Kids—The Heart of a Superkid—God's Character in You

ISBN 978-1-60463-070-1   30-1067

Kenneth Copeland Publications
Fort Worth, TX 76192-0001

For more information about Kenneth Copeland Ministries, call 1-800-600-7395 or visit kcm.org.

SuperkidAcademy.com • 1-800-606-4190

TABLE OF CONTENTS

WELCOME!

Dear Parent/Teacher,

I believe you will experience great and exciting things as you begin the faith adventure of *Superkid Academy Home Bible Study for Kids—The Heart of a Superkid—God's Character in You.*

As you launch into this faith-building time with your family or small group, take the opportunity to seek the Lord's direction about how to minister these lessons for maximum impact. God's Word does not return to Him void, and He will see to it that your children are BLESSED and grow strong in faith as you step out in His Anointing to teach them about Him.

Please keep in mind that we are praying for you. We believe and release our faith for a powerful anointing on you as you teach and impart His wisdom, and that your Superkids are strong in the Lord and mighty for Him.

Remember that we here at Academy Headquarters want to be a resource for you. Make sure you are in our contact base so we can keep in touch. And, let us know how we can better serve you and your Superkids.

We love you and look forward to hearing from you!

Love,

Commander Kellie

Commander Kellie

ACKNOWLEDGMENTS

Thank You, Lord, for Your love for our children. Thank You for the good life You have created for them. And, thank You for allowing us to teach Your children using Superkid Academy Curriculum.

There are many people who have made *The Heart of a Superkid—God's Character in You* a reality.

Personally, I'd like to acknowledge my family's support while writing, editing and compiling. Thank you to my wonderful husband, Stephen, for your faithful encouragement and love. You always make me look good! Thank you to my children for always being willing to help me—no matter what I ask! Rachel, Caleb, Lyndsey, Jenny and Max, you inspire me. Emily, you inspire me all over again. Just wait—you'll love being a Superkid, too!

Thank you, Mother and Daddy, for believing in me and for teaching me the uncompromised Word of God so that I can teach the Superkids!

The executive and senior management teams at KCM have backed this project regardless of cost, requiring excellence from us all. Thank you, John Copeland, James Tito, Stephen Swisher, Jan Harbour, Carleen Higgins, Marie Harrill, Cindy Hames and Michael Evans for bringing your supply and that of your departments.

Lu Eason, you did a great job of pulling all the pieces together. I like to call Lu: "Abso-Lu-tely!" She gets things done!

Our writing team was superb in so many ways. Foremost, I thank Lyndsey Swisher. You wrote with the pen of the Holy Spirit, taking each lesson and pulling out of it all the fun and creative elements a Superkid loves. Without your gift where would we be? Thank You, Lord, for Lyndsey!

Kim and Kiley Stephenson also played a great role in writing fun segments. Kim is always ready to jump into any adventure with me. Kim, you are an amazing and anointed ministry partner. And Kiley, you are definitely following in your mother's footsteps. You've gone from game cutie to game creator. I love having a real Superkid on the writing team!

Don Harris, known around here as Captain Don, is every commander's dream volunteer. Thank you for bringing your talents to Superkid Academy, worldwide. Jenny Kutz, you definitely know what makes a fun segment. Thank you for adding your creative juices to the mix. Chris and Gena Maselli, you are a blessing to this ministry. Thank you for your work on SKA.

Thank you, again, to all the departments for your tireless support. It always amazes me when I stop to think of the pool of talent that the Lord has brought to KCM. We have the BEST! But you are more than just talented—your passion for ministry is so powerful. I love you because you see all the way through this project to the little child sitting in his seat learning that JESUS is not only Lord, He's FUN! You will have many Superkids to your credit in heaven.

I love you all!

Commander Kellie

Commander Kellie

LEADING YOUR SUPERKID ACADEMY:
A SIMPLE GUIDE FOR HOME USE

We are excited you have brought Superkid Academy into your living room with the Home Bible Study for Kids! This powerful, Bible-based curriculum will guide your children into building a strong, personal relationship with the Lord and inspire them to live extraordinary, faith-filled lives.

Each of the 13 weeks provide five days of lessons, including:

- **Lesson Introduction from Commander Kellie:** Creator of Superkid Academy, with more than 20 years' experience ministering to children, Kellie Copeland Swisher has a unique anointing and perspective for reaching children with the uncompromised Word of God. Now, you and your family can benefit from her wisdom and experience through these timeless segments!
- **Lesson Outline:** Each lesson contains three main points, sub-points and supporting scriptures to empower you to clearly communicate these truths to your children.
- **Memory Verse:** Throughout the week, your children will have the opportunity to memorize and understand a scripture. More than that, they'll learn how to apply it directly to their lives!
- **Bible Lesson:** Bible lessons reinforce the memory verse and the principle behind them. Discussion questions open the way to further comprehension and will help you assess the lesson's impact in your children's lives.
- **Giving Lesson:** Each week, you will have the opportunity to teach your children the importance of tithing and giving so they can be "blessed to be a blessing" in the Body of Christ.
- **Game Time:** Games reinforce the message and give the whole family an occasion to celebrate what they've learned in a fun way.
- **Activity Sheet:** Activity sheets reinforce the lesson and provide application through crosswords, word searches, mazes and other puzzles.
- **Supplements:** To support the memory verse and lesson, two supplements from the following list are included each week:

    o **Object Lesson:** Illustrates the focus of the lesson and provides visual and hands-on elements to the teaching.

    o **Real Deal:** Highlights a historical person, place or event that exemplifies the lesson's theme.

    o **Storybook Theater or Read-Aloud:** Reinforces the message in creative, read-aloud stories.

    o **Food Fun:** Takes you and your children into the kitchen where you will discuss, illustrate and experience God's truth, using everyday items.

    o **Academy Lab:** Brings the lesson and science together.

And there's more! The enclosed Praise and Worship CD includes original, upbeat, kid-friendly songs that put the Word in your children's minds and hearts. The CD can be used around the house or in the car. And the karaoke, sing-along tracks allow your kids to sing their favorite songs—unaccompanied!

Making the Curriculum Work for Your Family

Superkid Academy's Home Bible Study for Kids gives you the flexibility to teach your children in a way that works for you! Each week's lesson is divided into five days of teaching. But, no two families—or their schedules—are alike. So, adjust the lessons to meet your needs. Use all five days of lessons, or select only a few to cover each week.

Whether you're using Superkid Academy's Home Bible Study for Kids as part of your homeschool curriculum, as a boost to your family devotions or in a weekly small group, you have the flexibility to make it work for you!

A Homeschool Bible Curriculum

Superkid Academy's Home Bible Study for Kids is easy to use, flexible and interactive—no dry Bible lessons here! It's ideal for a variety of learning styles. Each of the 13 weeks contains five days of lessons: a Bible Lesson, Giving Lesson, Game Time and two other lessons or stories to support the week's message. Choose all five lessons or the ones that best fit your educational structure. Optional Variations for several of the lessons have been included to meet a variety of needs.

Each week's Lesson Outline provides the major points, memory verse and a list supplies needed for the week, making it easy for busy families to prepare and customize lessons. Here are just a few additional ideas for tailoring the lessons for your homeschool:

- Re-read the Bible passage daily, throughout the week, to give your children—and you—time to meditate on the highlighted scripture
- Use one or more of the discussion questions as a journaling exercise
- Begin a weekly, family Game Night
- Use the Storybook Theater or Read-Aloud lesson in your nighttime routine

Family Devotions

Superkid Academy's Home Bible Study for Kids provides a powerful tool for you to disciple your children and teach them the Word of God in an easy, fun way. Use all five days' lessons, or select only a few. Each takes less than 15 minutes—an easy fit for busy schedules!

Lessons are numbered 1-5, allowing flexibility to select and fit them into your work schedules, church commitments and extra-curricular activities.

Here are two sample schedules:

5-Day Schedule

Sunday – Church (no lesson)

Monday – Bible Lesson

Tuesday – Object Lesson

Wednesday – Mid-week services (no lesson)

Thursday – Giving Lesson

Friday – Storybook Theater

Saturday - Game Time

3-Day Schedule

Sunday – Church (no lesson)

Monday – Bible Lesson

Tuesday – Soccer practice (no lesson)

Wednesday – Giving Lesson

Thursday – Soccer practice (no lesson)

Friday – Object Lesson

Saturday – Family time (no lesson)

A Weekly Small Group

Each week of Superkid Academy's Home Bible Study for Kids is designed for use over several days, but a week's worth of lessons can be easily consolidated for a small group. Simply choose the lessons that work best for your location and schedule, and allow additional time for discussion and prayer.

Sample Small Group Schedule

6 p.m.	Bible Lesson with discussion time
6:30 p.m.	Giving Lesson
6:45 p.m.	Object Lesson and prayer time
7:15 p.m.	Game Time
7:30 p.m.	Refreshments
7:45 p.m.	Closing

We're excited about how God will use Superkid Academy's Home Bible Study for Kids to mightily impact you and your family for His Kingdom! May God bless you as you disciple your children in the things that matter to Him. Proverbs 22:6 says, "Train up a child in the way he should go, and when he is old he will not depart from it." At Superkid Academy, we are confident that God will bless your efforts and that you and your children will see the reality of THE BLESSING in all you do!

Love,

Commander Kellie

Commander Kellie

HEALTH & SAFETY DISCLAIMER FOR "SUPERKID ACADEMY CURRICULUM"

Superkid Academy is a ministry of Eagle Mountain International Church, aka Kenneth Copeland Ministries (hereafter "EMIC"). The "Superkid Academy Curriculum" (hereafter "SKA Curriculum") provides age-appropriate teaching material to be used in the religious instruction of children. The SKA Curriculum includes physical activities that the children and leaders may participate in. Before engaging in any of the physical activities, participants should be in good physical condition as determined by their healthcare provider. EMIC is not responsible for injuries resulting from the implementation of activities suggested within the SKA Curriculum. Prior to implementing the SKA Curriculum, you should carefully review your organization's safety and health policies and make your own determination if the SKA Curriculum is appropriate for your organization's intended use.

By purchasing the SKA Curriculum, I, individually and/or as authorized representative for my organization, hereby agree to release, defend, hold harmless, and covenant not to sue EMIC, its Officers, Deacons, Ministers, Directors, Employees, Volunteers, Contractors, Staff, Affiliates, Agents, and Attorneys (collectively, the "EMIC Parties"), and the property of EMIC for any claim, including claims for negligence and gross negligence of any one or more of the EMIC Parties, arising out of my use or organization's use of and participation in the SKA Curriculum, participation in the suggested activities contained within the SKA Curriculum, or resulting from first-aid treatment or services rendered as a result of or in connection with the activities or participation in the activities.

WEEK 1: IT'S ALL GOOD

Memory Verse: *Then God looked over all he had made, and he saw that it was very good!* —Genesis 1:31

WEEK 1: SNAPSHOT   IT'S ALL GOOD

DAY	TYPE OF LESSON	LESSON TITLE	SUPPLIES
Day 1	Bible Lesson	Creation: Genesis 1	None
Day 2	Object Lesson	Watch It Grow	1-2 Cards per child of instant sponge animals in dissolving capsules (available inexpensively at dollar stores, toy stores or online), Clear container, Water
Day 3	Giving Lesson	Don't Come Empty-Handed	Small bouquet of fresh-cut flowers
Day 4	Real Deal	Walt Disney®	Mickey Mouse® or Minnie Mouse® attire, Mouse ears/tail, Face painted to look like mouse face, Disney® gloves
Day 5	Game Time	Creation Quick Draw	2 Large notepads, 2 Black markers (or pencils), 10 Slips of paper, 1 Bowl
Bonus	Activity Page	Creation Acrostic	1 Copy for each child

Lesson Introduction:

It's easy to teach children that God made trees, grass and flowers. But, how far short this falls from the grand planning and intricate details our heavenly Father invested in this place we know as Earth! He did so much for us, but do we know why?

- Why did God put so much detail into the countless colors of fish in the sea?
- What purpose could there be for the variety of flowers we see?

On the practical side, we can find no reason or definite purpose. But, if we understand the love of God, we realize the reason for His extravagance is to "wow" us! He wants us to see His great love through His Creation. The heavens declare His handiwork, His thoughtfulness and His great love for His kids! He placed man in a beautiful, extraordinary garden that was BLESSED! Adam and Eve didn't have to toil, but only obey and take their authority there.

Whenever I talk about THE BLESSING and the plan of God, I call it "The Sweet Life": an amazing life God has planned for you and your children. And, because you put Him in charge, He makes things work out for you and blesses everything you do (Romans 8; Deuteronomy 28)!

I like to talk about it every chance I get!

Love,

Commander Kellie

Commander Kellie

Lesson Outline:

This week, your children will learn about God's Creation, but you will move beyond the details of what God created and dig into the truth of *why* He created it—because He loves us!

I. BECAUSE HE LOVES US, HE MADE EVERYTHING GOOD

a. God created a wonderful planet called Earth.

b. He wanted a special home for His family.

c. God always thinks BIG for His kids.

d. He didn't rest or stop creating until He thought it was good enough for His kids!
Genesis 1:10, 12, 17-18, 21, 25, 31, 2:18

II. GOD PLANTED THE MOST BEAUTIFUL GARDEN IN THE WORLD Genesis 1:26-31

a. God put Adam and Eve in charge of the whole place. Verses 26-27

b. He gave His kids THE BLESSING to run everything! Verse 28

c. Our heavenly Father planted a spectacular Garden and made it grow! Verses 29-31; Genesis 2:8-12

d. There was no toil or hard work—THE BLESSING did the work. They just had to watch over it. Genesis 2:15

III. OUR HEAVENLY FATHER WANTED "THE SWEET LIFE" FOR HIS KIDS

a. Adam and Eve's lives in the Garden show us God's good plan for us, too. Ephesians 2:10 AMP

b. We were made to be exactly like Him. Genesis 1:26

c. God is the King of everything, and He wants His kids to rule like kings, too.

d. Our Father's plan for us was all good. We call it "The Sweet Life!" Jeremiah 29:11

Notes: _____

_____

_____

_____

_____

_____

_____

DAY 1: BIBLE LESSON — CREATION: GENESIS 1

Memory Verse: *Then God looked over all he had made, and he saw that it was very good!* — Genesis 1:31

This week, your family will read the story of Creation. Take this time to teach about God's glorious, creative work and His love for His children. All God's creation was—*and is*—good! Just as God created the Garden of Eden for His first children, Adam and Eve, He continues to create good things for His kids, today. Your children have a hope and a future (Jeremiah 29:11) because of all the good things God has created for them. Remind them of how much God loves them, and that He is still creating "The Sweet Life" for them!

Read Genesis 1: 1-31:
The Account of Creation

In the beginning God created the heavens and the earth. The earth was formless and empty, and darkness covered the deep waters. And the Spirit of God was hovering over the surface of the waters.

Then God said, "Let there be light," and there was light. And God saw that the light was good. Then he separated the light from the darkness. God called the light "day" and the darkness "night."

And evening passed and morning came, marking the first day.

Then God said, "Let there be a space between the waters, to separate the waters of the heavens from the waters of the earth." And that is what happened. God made this space to separate the waters of the earth from the waters of the heavens. God called the space "sky."

And evening passed and morning came, marking the second day.

Then God said, "Let the waters beneath the sky flow together into one place, so dry ground may appear." And that is what happened. God called the dry ground "land" and the waters "seas." And God saw that it was good. Then God said, "Let the land sprout with vegetation—every sort of seed-bearing plant, and trees that grow seed-bearing fruit. These seeds will then produce the kinds of plants and trees from which they came." And that is what happened. The land produced vegetation—all sorts of seed-bearing plants, and trees with seed-bearing fruit. Their seeds produced plants and trees of the same kind. And God saw that it was good.

And evening passed and morning came, marking the third day.

Then God said, "Let lights appear in the sky to separate the day from the night. Let them be signs to mark the seasons, days, and years. Let these lights in the sky shine down on the earth." And that is what happened. God made two great lights—the larger one to govern the day, and the smaller one to govern the night. He also made the stars. God set these lights in the sky to light the earth, to govern the day and night, and to separate the light from the darkness. And God saw that it was good.

And evening passed and morning came, marking the fourth day.

Then God said, "Let the waters swarm with fish and other life. Let the skies be filled with birds of every kind." So God created great sea creatures and every living thing that scurries and swarms in the water, and every sort of bird—each producing offspring of the same kind. And God saw that it was good. Then God blessed them, saying, "Be fruitful and multiply. Let the fish fill the seas, and let the birds multiply on the earth."

And evening passed and morning came, marking the fifth day.

Then God said, "Let the earth produce every sort of animal, each producing offspring of the same kind—livestock, small animals that scurry along the ground, and wild animals." And that is what happened. God made all sorts of wild animals, livestock, and small animals, each able to produce offspring of the same kind. And God saw that it was good.

Then God said, "Let us make human beings in our image, to be like us. They will reign over the fish in the sea, the birds in the sky, the livestock, all the wild animals on the earth, and the small animals that scurry along the ground."

So God created human beings in his own image. In the image of God he created them; male and female he created them.

Then God blessed them and said, "Be fruitful and multiply. Fill the earth and govern it. Reign over the fish in the sea, the birds in the sky, and all the animals that scurry along the ground."

Then God said, "Look! I have given you every seed-bearing plant throughout the earth and all the fruit trees for your food. And I have given every green plant as food for all the wild animals, the birds in the sky, and the small animals that scurry along the ground—everything that has life." And that is what happened.

Then God looked over all he had made, and he saw that it was very good!

And evening passed and morning came, marking the sixth day.

Discussion Questions:

Note: Answers will vary, but use this time of discussion to make sure your children understand the passage.

1. What are three things that happened in this passage?

2. What are some things this passage tells us that God created?
Answers will vary—animals, sun, moon, earth, sky, stars, oceans, etc.

3. What did God see when He looked at His Creation?
God saw that it was good. He said, "It is good" seven times in this passage. Verses 4, 10, 12, 17-18, 21, 25 and 31

4. What does this passage tell us about how we were made?
We were made in His image. We were made to be like Him.

5. If we are part of God's Creation, and if His Creation is good, then what does that say about us?
We were created, and we are good! We are unique and designed by God.

6. To whom did God give His Creation?
God gave His Creation to His children Adam and Eve.

Verses 28-30 say, "Then God blessed them and said, 'Be fruitful and multiply. Fill the earth and govern it. Reign over the fish in the sea, the birds in the sky, and all the animals that scurry along the ground.' Then God said, 'Look! I have given you every seed-bearing plant throughout the earth and all the fruit trees for your food. And I have given every green plant as food for all the wild animals, the birds in the sky, and the small animals that scurry along the ground—everything that has life.' And that is what happened."

7. What good things has God created for us today?
Answers will vary. Encourage your children to look at all the good things in their lives—a family that loves them, good health, a safe and loving home, the opportunity to know Jesus, friends, toys, etc.

8. Why does God create good things for us?
God loves us, and He loves to give to His children. He planned The Sweet Life for us. Jeremiah 29:11 says, "'For I know the plans I have for you,' says the Lord. 'They are plans for good and not for disaster, to give you a future and a hope.'"

Variation: Journaling

Consider using questions 7 and 8 as a journaling exercise to provide an opportunity for your children to practice their writing skills, chart their own faith journey and begin a prayer/study journal. In time, they can reread their entries and reflect on God's faithfulness and goodness to them.

Notes: _____

DAY 2: OBJECT LESSON [WATCH IT GROW]

Suggested Time: 5-7 minutes

Memory Verse: *Then God looked over all he had made, and he saw that it was very good!* — Genesis 1:31

Supplies: ☐ 1-2 Cards per child of instant sponge animals in dissolving capsules (available inexpensively at dollar stores, toy stores or online), Clear container partially filled with water

Lesson Instructions:

It's fun to go to the zoo to see the animals, isn't it? But we don't have to go to the zoo today to see some of the animals God made. At the store the other day, I found these "instant animals." The instructions say all you have to do is put them in water and within just a few minutes, your animals will "grow"! Let's give it a try.

Can you help me put these animals in the water? *(Give your child one or two instant animal capsules to drop into the container with the water.)*

OK, when I say, "A-a-a-a-animals, grow!" I want you to drop an animal capsule into the water. Ready? "A-a-a-a-animals, grow!" *(Watch as your child drops the capsules into the water.)*

That is so cool! And, I've got to admit, it's pretty fun to say, "Grow!" and things grow.

But, that's nothing compared to the kinds of things that happened in the earth when God spoke. When God spoke, He didn't even need to have a water container like ours. He just used His words and created the most beautiful animals you could ever imagine! Listen to Genesis 1:19-25:

And evening passed and morning came, marking the fourth day.

Then God said, "Let the waters swarm with fish and other life. Let the skies be filled with birds of every kind." So God created great sea creatures and every living thing that scurries and swarms in the water, and every sort of bird—each producing offspring of the same kind. And God saw that it was good. Then God blessed them, saying, "Be fruitful and multiply. Let the fish fill the seas, and let the birds multiply on the earth."

And evening passed and morning came, marking the fifth day.

Then God said, "Let the earth produce every sort of animal, each producing offspring of the same kind—livestock, small animals that scurry along the ground, and wild animals." And that is what happened. God made all sorts of wild animals, livestock, and small animals, each able to produce offspring of the same kind. And God saw that it was good.

God's Garden where He put the animals wasn't some tiny, little one that could fit on the top of this table. The whole Earth filled up with every kind of grass, bush, vine, plant and fruit tree, animal, fish and bird. It must have been absolutely amazing! When it was all finished, God even said it was really good. When God says it's really good, it's something else!

The greatest part of all is the fact that God didn't create that spectacular Garden just to show off. He created all that good stuff for Adam and Eve, His kids. The Bible says that God is the same yesterday, today and forever. That means if 'way back then, He created good stuff for His kids, He is still doing it now. Want to get in on the good stuff? All you have to do is be in God's family and go for The Sweet Life. Just water your mind, spirit and life with God's Word, and watch the blessings grow!

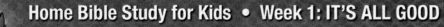

Variation No. 1: Nature Walk

Consider taking your children for a nature walk. Talk about how much you love the garden and how much you appreciate all that it provides—beautiful flowers, delicious fruits and vegetables and/or herbs. Talk about how much patience it takes and how you wish you could just speak to it and have it produce instantly, like in the Garden of Eden. You can then connect with the lesson by reading Genesis 1:11-12.

Variation No. 2: Zoo Visit

Plan a trip to the zoo. Connect with the lesson by talking about how God made the animals and how much you appreciate all the intricate details of His Creation. Discuss how amazing it is that God spoke and something as beautiful as a parrot or as huge and varied as an elephant or a rhinoceros came into being. Let your children know that God has given *them* the ability to call those things that be not as though they were (Romans 4:17) into their own lives, by speaking words of faith—just like God did!

Notes: _____

_____

_____

_____

_____

_____

_____

_____

_____

_____

_____

_____

_____

_____

_____

_____

_____

_____

_____

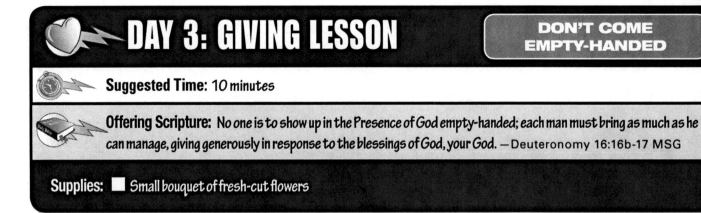

DAY 3: GIVING LESSON

DON'T COME EMPTY-HANDED

Suggested Time: 10 minutes

Offering Scripture: No one is to show up in the Presence of God empty-handed; each man must bring as much as he can manage, giving generously in response to the blessings of God, your God. —Deuteronomy 16:16b-17 MSG

Supplies: ☐ Small bouquet of fresh-cut flowers

Lesson Instructions:

Do you remember the last time we went to someone's house for dinner? We were on our best behavior, weren't we? We said, "Please" and "Thank you." Those are good manners, but there's something else we can do when we go to someone's house for dinner: We can bring a hostess gift.

A hostess gift is something you bring with you to a dinner or a party, like these flowers. You would give these flowers to the person who invited you to thank them for inviting you to dinner. This is a custom you don't see often, but it's a very thoughtful thing to do.

Did you know that the Bible tells us we should bring a kind of "hostess gift" to God? In Deuteronomy 16:16b-17 it says: "No one is to show up in the Presence of God empty-handed; each man must bring as much as he can manage, giving generously in response to the blessings of God, your God."

God has invited us to come into His house, to be close to Him. It would be a good idea to make sure we don't come empty-handed. Not because we owe Him something, but because He is always so generous to us and looking for ways to bless us. We bring Him gifts just to say thanks! Should we get an offering ready to bring to our amazing God this next Sunday? Let's get it now, and we'll take it with us the next time we attend service.

Notes: _____

_____

_____

_____

_____

_____

_____

_____

_____

_____

_____

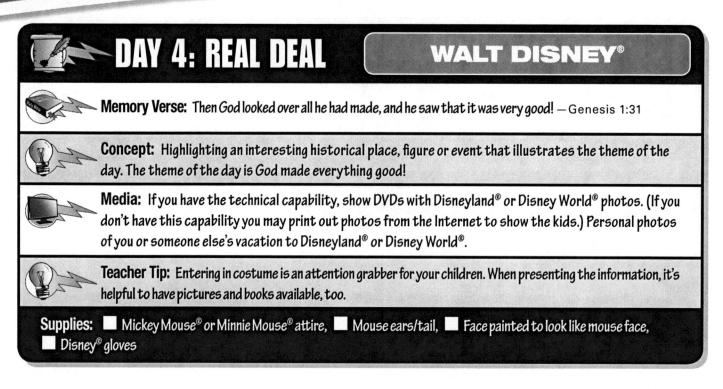

Intro:

Today, you will highlight an important historical figure for your children. Bring your message to life in practical terms—allow the children to see God's creative power at work in the world today.

Lesson Instructions:

This week, we've been talking about all the good things God has made for us. Can you remind me of our memory verse?

Then God looked over all he had made, and he saw that it was very good! —Genesis 1:31

In the beginning, God created the Garden of Eden for Adam and Eve to enjoy, and He filled it with lots of good things—food to eat, animals, and beautiful plants and trees. It took an amazing amount of creativity to make such a wonderful and perfect place.

Did you know that God gave us the ability to be creative, too? Think about the things that people enjoy today. Do they require creativity? How about amusement parks?

In the 1920s and '30s amusement parks with rides were mostly dirty places, not safe for families: NOT at all good. So in 1923, a 21-year-old man set out to change all that and revolutionize the amusement-park business, forever. His goal? To create a theme park that had fun attractions and a beautiful atmosphere—one that would stay clean and safe, but would keep changing with imagination.

He also created a famous cartoon character with some interesting features like ours. Can you guess who it is?

About Walt Disney®:

This man had one of the biggest imaginations of his time. His name was Walt Disney®. To this day, his name represents imagination, optimism, success and excellence.

Walt Disney® became interested in art at a very young age. He would even sell his sketches and drawings to neighbors to earn spending money.

Mr. Disney started his own business drawing advertisements and illustrations. Then, he launched an animation studio. At the age of 22, he started producing short, animated films. One of his good creations was a mouse called Mortimer—later named Mickey, or Mickey Mouse®. Just a few years later, other good things were created by Walt Disney®—Snow White and the Seven Dwarfs®, Pinocchio® and Bambi®. He also created books with some favorite Disney characters like Mickey and Minnie Mouse®, Donald Duck® and Pluto® the dog.

A Good Idea—Disneyland®:

Disneyland® was Walt Disney's® dream. For years he dreamed of building a "little family park" where parents could take their children for a day of fun. Now, that's a good idea!

Walt Disney® wanted to build his park and call it "The Happiest Place on Earth®." He said Disneyland® was a work of love. He wanted to make a place so good it would make dreams come true every day. Cast members at the park today, still hold true to the promise of turning the ordinary into the extraordinary!

How Good Is It?

Opening Day:

Disneyland® was opened to the public in July 1955. Amazingly, it was built in a little over a year! It cost about $17 million to build. The excitement of the grand opening was all over America.

The Lands:

Walt Disney® wanted to build separate areas inside Disneyland® so guests would feel like they were traveling from one land to another. He created this by transforming colors, textures and shapes of everything—even the trash cans! In the beginning, there were only five different theme "Lands":

- Main Street U.S.A.® —an early 20th century Midwest town
- Adventureland®—jungle-themed adventures
- Frontierland®—the Western frontier
- Fantasyland®—transforming cartoons into reality
- Tomorrowland®—looking into the future

Entertainment:

Every day there are parades, special shows, characters walking about, bands playing and fireworks! In the winter, snow is even made to fall several times a day.

Then and Now:

Many things have changed since Disneyland® opened in 1955.

- **THEN:** 20,000 people arrived on opening day.

- **NOW:** 65,000 people *per day* visit the park (That's 10-12 million visitors per year.)! 250 million people have visited Disneyland®—including presidents, kings and queens, and royalty from all over the globe.

- **THEN:** Ticket prices were $1 for admission. Individual tickets for 18 rides were 10-35 cents each.

- **NOW:** Tickets cost $80 for adults and $74 for children under 10.

- **THEN:** The park was closed Monday-Tuesday, during off-seasons.

- **NOW:** The parks are open year-round.

Making History:

Walt Disney® used his creativity to accomplish his dream and finish what he imagined. Now, millions of people get to enjoy what he called "The Happiest Place on Earth®."

Outro:

However, nothing is better than what God created for us from the very beginning—a place to live, have fun and enjoy "The Sweet Life." God is still in the creation business, and when HE plans it, IT'S ALL GOOD!

Notes: _____

_____

_____

_____

_____

_____

_____

_____

_____

_____

_____

_____

_____

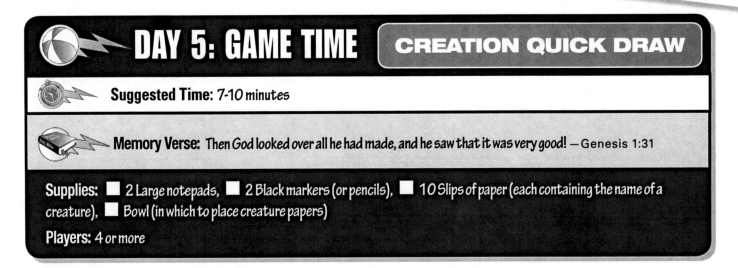

DAY 5: GAME TIME — CREATION QUICK DRAW

Suggested Time: 7-10 minutes

Memory Verse: Then God looked over all he had made, and he saw that it was very good! —Genesis 1:31

Supplies: ☐ 2 Large notepads, ☐ 2 Black markers (or pencils), ☐ 10 Slips of paper (each containing the name of a creature), ☐ Bowl (in which to place creature papers)

Players: 4 or more

Below is a list of creatures for the Creation Quick Draw. Feel free to add your own ideas:

1. Fish	6. Lion
2. Rabbit	7. Snake
3. Giraffe	8. Bird
4. Rhinoceros	9. Butterfly
5. Deer	10. Spider

Prior to Game:

Write one creature name on each slip of paper. Place the papers in the bowl. Divide your family into two teams and take seats around a table.

Game Instructions:

Choose one player from each team to be the artist. Have one artist pick a creature paper from the bucket and show it to the other artist.

On "Ready, Set, Draw!" the artists must draw the creature listed. As they draw, their teammates will shout out answers, trying to correctly identify the creature. The first team to correctly guess the creature gets 100 points. Choose new artists, and play another round.

Game Goal:

Continue until one team reaches 500 points.

Final Word:

Some of the creatures drawn looked pretty strange, didn't they? Isn't it amazing to think that God created each one of them perfectly the very first time?! He didn't even need an eraser!

Variation: Single Artist

For fewer than four players, have only one artist. All players will take turns drawing while the other players try to guess which animal is being drawn. Award points to the player who guesses the right answer. Each correct guess earns 100 points. The first player to earn 500 points, wins.

Notes: _____

_____

_____

_____

_____

_____

_____

_____

_____

_____

_____

_____

_____

_____

_____

_____

_____

_____

_____

_____

_____

_____

_____

_____

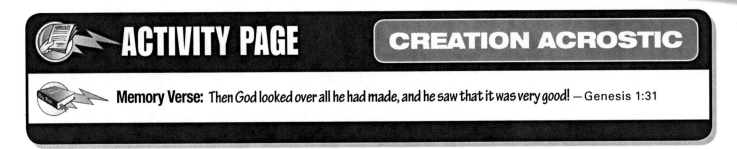

ACTIVITY PAGE · CREATION ACROSTIC

Memory Verse: *Then God looked over all he had made, and he saw that it was very good!* — Genesis 1:31

In Genesis 1, we saw that God created many good things for Adam and Eve, and ultimately, for you. Using the provided words, fill in the puzzle spaces below. Remember, the words will fit together in only one correct way.

Animals   Birds   Earth   Fish

Fruit   Heavens   Livestock Moon

Trees   Sea   Sun   Sky

ANSWER KEY

Notes: _____

_____

_____

_____

_____

_____

_____

_____

_____

_____

_____

_____

_____

_____

_____

_____

_____

_____

_____

WEEK 2: THE BIGGEST LIE

WEEK 2

Memory Verse: *The thief's purpose is to steal and kill and destroy.*—John 10:10a

WEEK 2: SNAPSHOT — THE BIGGEST LIE

DAY	TYPE OF LESSON	LESSON TITLE	SUPPLIES
Day 1	Bible Lesson	The Fall	None
Day 2	Object Lesson	Deal Breaker	1 Candy bar for each child, Beautifully wrapped box with something awful inside, like an old, dirty sock or banana peel
Day 3	Giving Lesson	Where Did It Come From, Really?	Board game for preschoolers, Work gloves, Rake, Broom, Trash can
Day 4	Storybook Theater	Davy's Deception	Whiteboard or chalkboard or easel with paper, Markers or pastel chalks, Rags (to blend chalks), Pencil and eraser (art pencils work best), Art smock. **Optional costumes/props:** Ball cap and wristwatch, Jeans, Sweatshirt, Glasses, Apron, Cookbook, Shirt and tie, Newspaper
Day 5	Game Time	Telephone	List of "Telephone" game phrases, Clipboard, Dark-colored sheet of paper
Bonus	Activity Page	Unscramble Creation	1 Copy for each child

Lesson Introduction:

Before you teach this lesson, take some time to think seriously about the conversation Satan had with Eve in the Garden. He lied to her on several different levels:

- First, he led her to think she could meet her own need for wisdom without God.

- Second, he told her she could be like God…but, SHE WAS ALREADY just like God! God's wisdom was available to Eve, but she chose Satan's way instead, to "know" good and evil. What a lie!

All Adam and Eve had known in the Garden was good, but by obeying Satan, they knew, or "became intimately acquainted with," a life filled with evil. Our kids need to understand how much the devil hates them and why. On the heels of this revelation, I like to ask them, "Why would you listen to and obey someone who hates you?"

This is also a great time to talk to your Superkids about listening to their parents, as Eve should have listened to hers. Satan led Eve to believe her Father was keeping something from her. He's trying to convince kids today their parents are doing the same thing to them. He's telling them, "Your parents just don't want you to have any fun," or, "They just don't understand."

Satan doesn't have any new tricks, so we're teaching our Superkids to be wise to all of them!

This week, leave the kids with a big cliffhanger. Next week…Jesus to the rescue!

Love,

Commander Kellie

Commander Kellie

Lesson Outline:

This week, you'll train your children to recognize and overcome the deceit of the enemy. Just as Satan wanted to keep Eve from enjoying THE BLESSING, he wants to keep your children from enjoying it, too. As you teach this lesson, remind your children of The Sweet Life God has for them. He loves them so much and only wants to give them the best!

I. A TRAITOR NAMED SATAN CAME INTO THE GARDEN OF EDEN Genesis 3

a. He was kicked out of heaven for treason. Luke 10:18

b. He said he was going to be like the Most High God. Isaiah 14:12-14

c. God made Adam and Eve in His own image, instead. They were just like God.

d. This made Satan mad, mad, mad! He's been trying to be like God ever since.

II. SATAN TOLD THE BIGGEST LIE EVER SO HE COULD STEAL THE BLESSING Genesis 3

a. God blessed Adam and Eve with more than they could have asked for—The Sweet Life.

b. Satan lied and told Eve that God was holding out on them. Verses 1-5

c. She believed the lie that she should eat the fruit. Verse 6

d. When Adam and Eve obeyed Satan's word, they let Satan be their god and traded God's BLESSING for a curse. Verses 7-8

e. God didn't curse Adam and Eve. Because they had joined with Satan, the curse was already in operation. God just explained what life would be like without THE BLESSING—HARD WORK! Verses 16-19

III. SATAN IS STILL LYING ABOUT GOD TODAY

a. Don't listen to Satan; there is no truth in him. John 8:44

b. Satan wants kids to think God doesn't care about them.

c. Satan doesn't want kids to know God loves them and has good things planned for them.

d. Our heavenly Father longed to have His family back in The Sweet Life!

Notes:_____

_____

_____

_____

DAY 1: BIBLE LESSON

THE FALL

Memory Verse: *The thief's purpose is to steal and kill and destroy.*—John 10:10a

As you continue with the story following Creation, this is a great opportunity to teach your children that God gave us this amazing gift and responsibility: the right to choose! He doesn't force Himself on us. Even in the beginning, He gave Adam and Eve the opportunity to choose to follow Him and live in THE BLESSING. That's still the wonderful privilege He allows today. He will never force us to be disciples, but He knows if we choose to become disciples, we will be BLESSED! His desire is for us to follow Him because we love Him and *want* to obey His plan for our lives.

Read Genesis 2:15-17 and 3:1-19:
The Fall of Man
Genesis 2:15-17

The Lord God placed the man in the Garden of Eden to tend and watch over it. But the Lord God warned him, "You may freely eat the fruit of every tree in the garden—except the tree of the knowledge of good and evil. If you eat its fruit, you are sure to die."

Genesis 3:1-19

The serpent was the shrewdest of all the wild animals the Lord God had made. One day he asked the woman, "Did God really say you must not eat the fruit from any of the trees in the garden?"

"Of course we may eat fruit from the trees in the garden," the woman replied. "It's only the fruit from the tree in the middle of the garden that we are not allowed to eat. God said, 'You must not eat it or even touch it; if you do, you will die.'"

"You won't die!" the serpent replied to the woman. "God knows that your eyes will be opened as soon as you eat it, and you will be like God, knowing both good and evil."

The woman was convinced. She saw that the tree was beautiful and its fruit looked delicious, and she wanted the wisdom it would give her. So she took some of the fruit and ate it. Then she gave some to her husband, who was with her, and he ate it, too. At that moment their eyes were opened, and they suddenly felt shame at their nakedness. So they sewed fig leaves together to cover themselves.

When the cool evening breezes were blowing, the man and his wife heard the Lord God walking about in the garden. So they hid from the Lord God among the trees. Then the Lord God called to the man, "Where are you?"

He replied, "I heard you walking in the garden, so I hid. I was afraid because I was naked."

"Who told you that you were naked?" the Lord God asked. "Have you eaten from the tree whose fruit I commanded you not to eat?"

The man replied, "It was the woman you gave me who gave me the fruit, and I ate it."

Then the Lord God asked the woman, "What have you done?"

"The serpent deceived me," she replied. "That's why I ate it."

Then the Lord God said to the serpent, "Because you have done this, you are cursed more than all animals, domestic and wild. You will crawl on your belly, groveling in the dust as long as you live. And I will cause hostility between you and the woman, and between your offspring and her offspring. He will strike your head, and you will strike his heel."

Then he said to the woman, "I will sharpen the pain of your pregnancy, and in pain you will give birth. And you will desire to control your husband, but he will rule over you."

And to the man he said, "Since you listened to your wife and ate from the tree whose fruit I commanded you not to eat, the ground is cursed because of you. All your life you will struggle to scratch a living from it. It will grow thorns and thistles for you, though you will eat of its grains. By the sweat of your brow will you have food to eat until you return to the ground from which you were made. For you were made from dust, and to dust you will return."

Discussion Questions:

1. Who are the main characters in today's passage?
Adam, Eve and Satan

2. What was the one "rule" that God made for Adam and Eve in the Garden?
They could not eat from the tree in the middle of the Garden.

3. Describe the serpent.
He was crafty and apparently did not crawl on his belly until after the curse came on him. Satan used him to say only part of what God actually said.

4. Did Eve trick Adam?
No, the Bible says Adam was there with her. He saw the whole thing and chose to disobey God's command!

5. What was the result of Adam and Eve's decision to disobey?
Adam and Eve and all their descendants became cursed because of their union with evil Satan. They had to be banished, or kicked out, of the Garden to keep them from eating from the Tree of Life and living forever in their cursed state, until God could send a Savior. They paid a huge price for their decision! Remember, Adam truly did have an opportunity to say no to the wrong choice, but he didn't!

6. What are some areas where you are tempted to disobey?
Accept all answers and even share some of your own.

7. How does disobedience make you feel?
Accept children's responses, and remind them that fear and disobedience are part of the curse from the Fall of Adam and Eve.

8. What can you learn from this story about Adam and Eve's disobedience?
Answers will vary, but here are possible choices:

- God wants me to obey, but He will not force me to make the right choice.

- There are consequences to my actions.

- Sin is never OK, although God wants me to confess my sins if I do make a mistake, and He will forgive my sins (1 John 1:9).

- Jesus crushed the serpent's head while He was on the cross, when He died for my sins!

Variation No. 1: Copy Work

Young children benefit greatly from copy work. It not only reinforces the Word of God in their lives, but also introduces them to quality writing, which, in turn, improves vocabulary, writing and composition skills. Consider having your children copy one or more verses from this passage into their prayer journals.

Variation No. 2: Journaling

Children may enjoy journaling or writing about a time when they were tempted to disobey but didn't, rather than discussing areas where obedience is difficult for them.

Notes: _____

_____

_____

_____

_____

_____

_____

_____

_____

_____

_____

_____

_____

_____

_____

_____

_____

_____

_____

_____

_____

_____

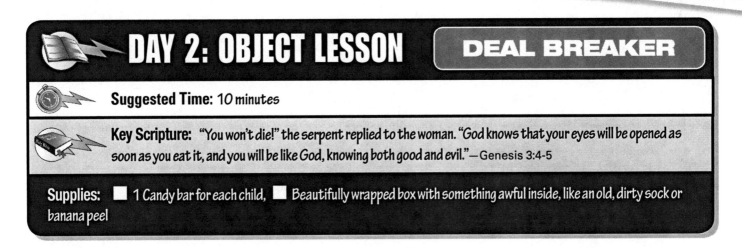

DAY 2: OBJECT LESSON — DEAL BREAKER

Suggested Time: 10 minutes

Key Scripture: "You won't die!" the serpent replied to the woman. "God knows that your eyes will be opened as soon as you eat it, and you will be like God, knowing both good and evil."—Genesis 3:4-5

Supplies: ☐ 1 Candy bar for each child, ☐ Beautifully wrapped box with something awful inside, like an old, dirty sock or banana peel

Lesson Instructions:

Here, Sweetheart, I have something for you. *(Give the candy bar to your child.)*

I know how much you like candy bars, so when I saw this, I just wanted you to have it. It looks good, doesn't it? *(Build up the idea that you have given your child something of worth, but don't be too obvious or you will tip them off when it comes time to trade.)*

You can eat that later, but I do have another option. I wonder if you might consider giving it back to me…to trade it for this beautiful present. *(Pull out the gift as you offer the trade.)*

What do you think? Would you like to have what's in this nicely wrapped box? *(Give them a minute or two to decide. Make the trade enticing because the trade will drive your point home. If your child trades, have them open the gift. If you have more than one child, be ready to make the same deal to the others.)*

Oh no! I guess that wasn't a good deal after all, was it?

That reminds me of someone else who didn't make a very good deal. In Genesis 3, the Bible tells us about Adam and Eve and the really good deal they had with God. They had a beautiful home in a garden that God planted for them, they got to walk and talk with God every evening, and they even had all kinds of wonderful food to eat. There were trees that always had ripe fruit for Adam and Eve to eat, anytime they wanted. But, Adam and Eve made a mistake. They believed the lies of the devil and messed up their deal with God. They traded all those good things away. Make sure you never trade what you know—that God is a good God—for the devil's lies!

Notes: _____

_____

_____

_____

_____

_____

_____

_____

Notes: _____

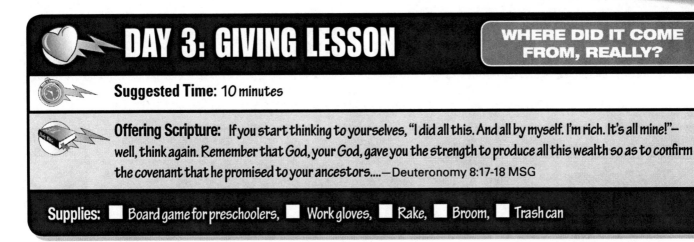

DAY 3: GIVING LESSON

WHERE DID IT COME FROM, REALLY?

Suggested Time: 10 minutes

Offering Scripture: If you start thinking to yourselves, "I did all this. And all by myself. I'm rich. It's all mine!"— well, think again. Remember that God, your God, gave you the strength to produce all this wealth so as to confirm the covenant that he promised to your ancestors....—Deuteronomy 8:17-18 MSG

Supplies: ☐ Board game for preschoolers, ☐ Work gloves, ☐ Rake, ☐ Broom, ☐ Trash can

Lesson Instructions:

Kids can't go out and get jobs in stores or restaurants, but there *are* ways that kids can earn money. Look at these things, and see if you can guess what kind of job a kid could do with them.

(Hold up the preschool game.) This is for young kids, but what does it make you think of? What kind of job do you think this would stand for? *(Allow for answers.)*

Right! Babysitting. Boys and girls can babysit to make extra money.

Here are some other items: a pair of gloves and a rake. What does this make you think of? *(more answers)*

Yard work. Kids can rake leaves, pull weeds or mow grass for extra cash.

My last two things are a broom and a trash can. What do these things represent? *(Get answers.)*

You guessed it, chores around the house, cleaning up and taking out the trash.

Have you ever noticed that when you start working for your money, it can be a little harder to give it away?

That makes me think of this verse in Deuteronomy: "If you start thinking to yourselves, 'I did all this. And all by myself. I'm rich. It's all mine!'—well, think again. Remember that God, your God, gave you the strength to produce all this wealth"; or you could say it this way—don't forget that God gave you two strong arms and two strong legs so that you can work and earn money. Secondly, remember He gives you the great ideas, and most importantly He gives you supernatural power to become wealthy.

This is a great reminder for us all. If we are tempted to be stingy with God, remember that He blessed us with healthy bodies and good minds. And, the next time you put your energy into making some money, don't forget to give back to the Lord who made you powerful in the first place!

Notes: _____

_____

_____

_____

_____

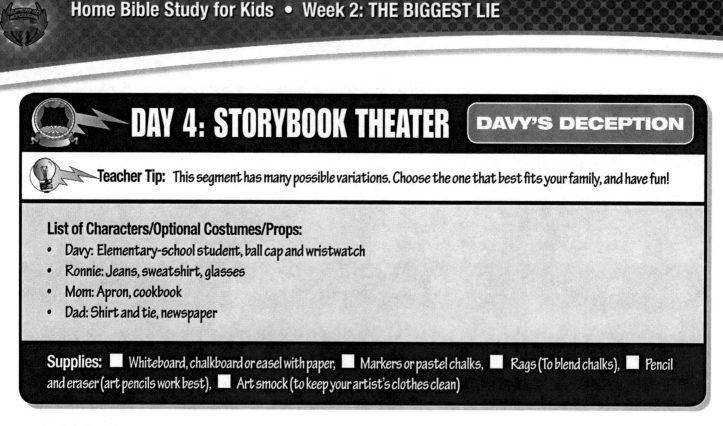

DAY 4: STORYBOOK THEATER — DAVY'S DECEPTION

Teacher Tip: This segment has many possible variations. Choose the one that best fits your family, and have fun!

List of Characters/Optional Costumes/Props:
- Davy: Elementary-school student, ball cap and wristwatch
- Ronnie: Jeans, sweatshirt, glasses
- Mom: Apron, cookbook
- Dad: Shirt and tie, newspaper

Supplies: ☐ Whiteboard, chalkboard or easel with paper, ☐ Markers or pastel chalks, ☐ Rags (To blend chalks), ☐ Pencil and eraser (art pencils work best), ☐ Art smock (to keep your artist's clothes clean)

Variation No. 1:

Read the story as part of your read-aloud time.

Variation No. 2:

Read the story like an old-time radio skit, complete with different actors for each part. If you are limited on participants, then allow more than one part per person and change the voice. Make copies of the skit, and have each actor highlight their lines.

Variation No. 3:

Act out the story as a fun skit. Perhaps your children can practice during the day (even creating fun costumes from everyday items) and then perform it in the evening for the whole family. Before beginning your skit, remember to introduce your cast!

Variation No. 4:

Create a storybook theater where one or more family members sketch the story on a whiteboard, chalkboard or artist's easel, as another member reads the story. Initially, there will be a few supplies to purchase, but don't let this be a deterrent from using the illustrated story option! Once the supplies have been purchased, they'll be long-lasting and reusable. Teacher tip: Cut the paper to fit on the board and tape it down. Lightly sketch the drawing with a pencil prior to presentation. Time may not allow for the picture to be completely drawn and colored during the story. Erase the pencil lines, so light lines are visible to you but not to your audience. Review the story ahead of time to determine the amount of time needed to complete the illustration while telling the story. When the story begins, use black markers to draw the picture, tracing your pencil lines. Next, apply color using the pastel chalk. Then, blend the color with the rags to complete the picture.

Story:

Davy looked at his new watch and wondered if it really kept time the way it should. His dad had brought it home two nights before and given it to Davy. He said he had bought it from the new store across the street from where he worked. The watch was certainly a good-looking one. It had a black wristband, with a dark blue border and a silver face that glowed when Davy turned the light off in his room. There were no numbers on it, which made it even cooler as far as Davy was concerned. Watches with the numbers on them were for babies.

The trouble was, school had just gotten out, and his new watch said it was almost 9:30. That was Davy's bedtime on a school night, and Davy was not nearly ready for bed, yet. The sun was still up. Davy decided he would have to ask his mom about this.

When he got home, Davy walked into the kitchen and threw his backpack on a chair.

"Hi, Sweetheart, how was school?" Davy's mom inquired.

Davy thought about this for a moment. His mom loved asking about school, and Davy tried to think of something extremely interesting to tell her, but nothing came to mind. Today, school had been pretty much just *school.* Nothing really exciting or dramatic had happened. While he was pondering this, Davy remembered the time when his best friend, Ronnie, had spilled his apple juice in the lunchroom. Now that was an exciting and memorable school day! Mr. Draper, the principal, just happened to be hurrying by. The timing was perfect; his feet hit the slippery drink on the hard tile floor, and in less than a second Mr. Draper landed flat on his back, knocking over three lunch trays and sending a couple of chairs flying. Principal Draper got to his feet unhurt and smiling, his suit freshly decorated with bits of lunch, and the whole room burst into applause. Ronnie jumped up on his chair and bowed to the cheering room, acknowledging their appreciation for his part in the excitement. Mr. Draper smiled at the cheering students, as though he had planned it all just for their entertainment. Thinking back on that happy occasion, Davy wondered why school couldn't be more like that all the time. Other than what had become known as the "Apple Juice Incident," school was usually fairly routine.

"I asked you how school was," Davy's mom repeated.

"Oh, great," Davy replied, "it was wonderful, awesome stuff. Mom, math was incredible."

"Davy, don't be a smart aleck," his mother warned.

"Aw, I'm just teasing," Davy grinned. "Can I go over to Ronnie's house?"

"Be home in time for dinner," she replied. "And, no apple juice!"

Davy grabbed a cookie from the counter and headed for the door.

"I like the way your new watch looks!" his mom said with a smile. "At least you'll know when it's time to leave Ronnie's and come home for dinner."

Davy held his wrist up so she could see the new timepiece. "With this watch, I might not be home until 2 in the morning," he replied. "Look at the time—it says it's after 9:30, now!"

Davy was not nearly as happy with his new gift as he had been this morning. His mother inspected the face of his watch. After just a moment, she looked up at her son and smiled.

"Davy, you are wearing your new watch upside down," his mother informed him. "The actual time is just after 3:00."

"I guess I need one that can't fake me out," Davy mumbled, glaring at the watch as though it had put itself on his wrist upside down.

On the way to Ronnie's house, Davy passed a poster that was stapled to a wooden fence. The word *contest* caught his eye. Davy stopped to see what contest was happening. "Twenty-First Annual Tall Tale Contest," the poster proclaimed. "Mystery Grand Prize will be awarded for the best 'whopper' told by any contestant." Davy had never heard of anything called a

"Tall Tale Contest" before. When he got to Ronnie's house Davy told him about the poster.

"What's a 'Tall Tale' contest?" he asked his friend. Ronnie smiled at Davy.

"You really don't know?" Ronnie asked. "It's a contest to see who can tell the biggest lie. You know—a story, a fable. Haven't you ever heard the word *whopper?*"

Davy had to think about this for a second. "Come to think about it, I did read the word *whopper* on the poster," Davy admitted.

"That's right," Ronnie went on, "that poster isn't talking about burgers, you know. In plain English, it's a lie-telling contest."

At that particular moment, Davy wasn't thinking too much about the lying part. He was too caught up in the idea of winning something awesome. The words *mystery* and *grand* were all that he could focus on. *I wonder what the mystery grand prize is,* Davy thought to himself. *It would be pretty cool to win something for my mom and dad.* Davy decided he would enter this contest and see if he could win the grand prize...whatever it was.

Ronnie rolled his eyes when Davy told him his plan. "You would be the worst contestant ever!" Ronnie scoffed. "You are the lousiest liar I know. In fact, I don't know if you have ever even told one!"

Davy thought about this for a moment. His friend might be right—Davy pretty much always told the truth, and it seemed like the easiest thing to do, too. Lying usually seemed complicated and dangerous.

"I could practice," Davy replied. "Maybe if I worked at it for a couple of days I might discover that it's a hidden talent."

Ronnie looked doubtful. "If I were you, I would forget about it. You don't even know what the prize is."

Davy looked at his watch, which looked like it said 10:30.

"It's 4:00. I have to go," said Davy. "I'll see you tomorrow at school, Ronnie."

On the way home, Davy tried to think of ways to practice telling a lie. In fact, he needed to tell a huge lie, an enormous lie. To win the mysterious grand prize, Davy would need to tell the biggest lie of all.

When he walked through the door, his mother told him that dinner was ready. Davy decided this would be a chance to practice, so he said the first thing that popped into his head.

"I already ate at Ronnie's. His mom cooked an early dinner and asked me to help eat it because she fixed so much."

Davy's mother smiled and exclaimed, "That was so sweet of her! What's awesome is that since you already ate, you will have more time to clean your room while your father and I are eating. I checked it today and it's a mess!"

Davy went to his room and looked around. It was a dump! About that time, the smell of barbecued hamburgers followed him, and Davy's stomach growled a protest.

Boy, I blew it! Davy thought to himself. *That was the stupidest lie I could have come up with!* By the time Davy finished straightening up his room, he was tired and VERY hungry.

Walking through the kitchen he saw that dinner was long-since over and his mom was just finishing the dishes.

Davy's father was reading the paper, and without putting it down he asked Davy, "How was your day today, Sport?"

Davy thought to himself for a moment, and then decided this was another great chance to practice telling a real "whopper." If he could fool his parents, he could probably beat a bunch of strangers.

"Dad, you may find this incredible, but I've never had a day like it." His dad looked over the top of his paper.

Davy thought for a moment and blurted, "We had a real interesting day. First we had fire, then we had water, then we had ice."

Davy immediately wondered where *that* idea came from, and thought of his missed dinner. Davy's dad put down his paper.

"I have got to hear about this," he said. "School was never quite that interesting when I was your age!"

Davy swallowed and felt desperate.

"Well, it all started when Paulie Madison took his glasses off during recess. We were playing tag, and he didn't want them to break, so he put them on top of his backpack. A few minutes later, Paulie's backpack was on fire!"

Davy's mom looked puzzled. "How did it catch on fire?" she asked.

Davy cleared his throat. "The glasses sort of acted like a magnifying glass and made a hot spot on Paulie's backpack, I guess," answered Davy.

"What about the water?" his father questioned. "I just have to hear about the water!"

"That's a little more complicated," said Davy. "The water was from a little fire extinguisher that was hanging on the wall by the playground. One of the teachers grabbed it and sprayed it toward the backpack."

Davy's dad assumed a relieved expression. "Well, that's good," he said. "Was Paulie upset about his backpack?"

Before Davy could answer, his mother spoke up. "I didn't know that fire extinguishers had water in them. Don't they have some sort of chemical or something?"

"You know, you're right," said Davy's dad. "They do put chemicals in those extinguishers, now that you mention it."

Davy felt exasperated. "This was an old one," Davy explained, "practically prehistoric, just like everything else in our school."

At this Davy's mom asked, "What about the ice? You said you had fire, water AND ice at school today."

Davy looked up, realizing he had one more "whopper" to tell. "Ah, yes, the ice," Davy stammered, thinking fast: *The ice...oh boy, the ice!*

At that precise moment, Davy's mind went completely blank. He could not think of one single ice story to make up. In fact, Davy realized he didn't even want to make up an ice story or any other story. This tall-tale-telling was exhausting!

"Davy," his dad said, "are you OK, son?"

Davy heaved a sigh and sat down with his back against the couch where his dad was sitting.

"Dad, can I tell you something?" Davy asked.

"I thought you already were," his father replied.

"Dad, what I mean is, I want to tell you what really happened today."

His dad looked at him, with his reading glasses perched on the end of his nose. "What is it, Davy?"

"Well, I made up all that stuff about school," Davy admitted.

Davy heard his mother's voice from the kitchen, where she had disappeared to a few minutes before.

"No fire?" she asked.

"Uh, no fire," Davy said.

"No water either?" his father questioned.

"Not even a drop," Davy answered.

Davy heard his parents say in unison, "No ice, I suppose."

Davy thought it was weird that sometimes a mom and dad would say the same thing at exactly the same time like that.

"Not even," said Davy. "But I did decide to enter a pretty stupid contest today."

Davy went on to tell his parents about the poster, the mysterious grand prize and even the nonexistent dinner at Ronnie's house. By the time he was finished explaining everything, Davy surprisingly felt much better.

Davy's dad patted the couch next to him and Davy sat down. "Son, I'm glad you wanted to win something for your mother and me," his father said. "What you probably did not realize is that no grand prize offer could be worth lying about."

He put his arm around Davy. "Here's what I want you to remember: Anything you have to lie about to win is no good. And there is one more thing too, son. The biggest lie was told about 6,000 years ago, and no one has topped it yet."

Davy looked up at his dad, who went on to say, "It all happened in the Garden of Eden, when a lying serpent told God's own children that He was not really such a good Father at all."

"You mean the devil!" Davy exclaimed.

"That's right," Davy's dad said. "God always tells the truth, and the devil always lies. It's pretty simple."

Davy spoke loud enough for his mom to hear. "No more contests for me," he declared. "No tall tales, whoppers or fables."

"One more thing, Mom and Dad," Davy continued. "I think you should probably bring on some serious correction for me because of lying like that."

Davy's mom looked surprised, and his dad smiled and nodded. "You beat me to it, son. I know exactly what you need." Davy's dad reached for his Bible and handed it to Davy. "We are going to spend some time in the Word together."

Davy took his father's Bible and with a deep breath, knowing that correction brings relief, he went with his dad. "Yes, sir," he replied. "That sounds like what I need to put in my brain and my heart!"

Later that evening, Davy's father put his arm around Davy's shoulder and said, "You never did really tell me about your day. How was school?"

"It was pretty good," Davy replied. "I found out how to tell time…backward!"

"Who showed you how to tell time backward?" His father asked, looking down at his son's new watch.

Davy glanced at his mother as she walked in from the kitchen.

"You might just say I was self-taught," he explained. Davy's mom just handed him a huge piece of apple pie and smiled.

Davy sat down and took a bite. "Thanks, Mom, you're the best!"

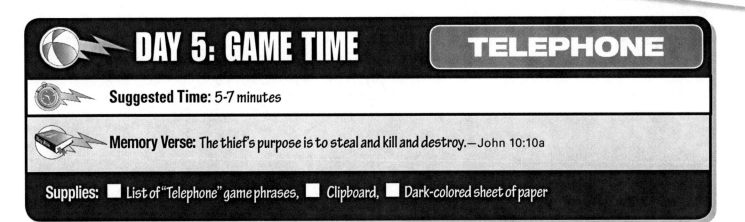

Telephone Game Phrases: Below is a list of phrases. Feel free to add some of your own.

1. The devil got kicked out of heaven for rebelling against God.

2. God made Adam and Eve just like Him.

3. Satan is a thief, and he was the first and worst liar ever!

4. God gave Adam and Eve a huge present—the planet Earth!

5. Satan lied to Adam and Eve about God.

6. God's family lost everything when they listened to Satan.

7. Everything changed—lions got mean, and work got hard.

8. With Jesus, we can stomp on the devil's head!

Prior to Game:

Place the "Telephone" game phrases on a clipboard and cover it with a colored sheet of paper, so the kids can't see it.

Game Instructions:

(Gather your family so that each person can easily whisper a phrase to the next person.) Who likes to talk on the telephone? *(Allow for answers.)* This game is called, "Telephone," but instead of talking on a telephone, you are each going to BE the telephone. Here's how…. Just like a telephone landline carries a message, you're going to carry a message! I'm going to whisper a sentence or phrase into one person's ear. Then, that person will whisper the phrase to the next, and so on, until the last person hears the message. That person will then tell us what the sentence or phrase is. We'll see if we can get it right, all the way around. Remember to whisper. No one else should hear you when you share it. I'll tell you if we got it right!

Game Goal:

For the phrase to be as close to the original as possible by the time it reaches the last person. Play as many rounds as you'd like.

Final Word:

Did you notice how easy it was for the phrase to get twisted? That's exactly what Satan tries to do to the truth: He tries to twist it. And, if we listen to lots of different people instead of finding God's truth in His Word, then we'll get mixed up, too. That's why we always need to be reading and listening to God's Word and the Holy Spirit.

Notes: _____

_____

_____

_____

_____

_____

_____

_____

_____

_____

_____

_____

_____

_____

_____

_____

_____

_____

_____

_____

_____

_____

_____

_____

_____

ACTIVITY PAGE — UNSCRAMBLE CREATION

Memory Verse: The thief's purpose is to steal and kill and destroy. —John 10:10a

Satan's goal is to bring confusion and strife into every situation he can. Thankfully, Jesus is the Master Unscrambler. Through Him, God set things right, restored our relationship with our heavenly Father and made it so that we could enjoy THE BLESSING. Now, it's your turn to unscramble these Creation words.

MADA = _ _ _ _

KAENS = _ _ _ _ _

DARGNE = _ _ _ _ _ _

LSSEBGNI = _ _ _ _ _ _ _ _

WLEODGKNE = _ _ _ _ _ _ _ _ _

VEE = _ _ _

ETRE = _ _ _ _

UCRES = _ _ _ _ _

VILE = _ _ _ _

ENED = _ _ _ _

ELI = _ _ _

Unscramble CREATION

ANSWER KEY

Notes: _____

_____

_____

_____

_____

_____

_____

_____

_____

_____

_____

_____

_____

_____

_____

_____

_____

WEEK 3: JESUS TO THE RESCUE

Memory Verse: The thief's purpose is to steal and kill and destroy. My purpose is to give them a rich and satisfying life. —John 10:10

WEEK 3: SNAPSHOT — JESUS TO THE RESCUE

DAY	TYPE OF LESSON	LESSON TITLE	SUPPLIES
Day 1	Bible Lesson	God's Plan to Get His Children Back	None
Day 2	Read-Aloud	Best-Case Scenario: "Rise to the Top"	None
Day 3	Giving Lesson	Who's Invited?	A birthday cake and candles
Day 4	Food Fun	Eggsplosion	Microwave oven, Small table, Medium-sized bowl, Mixing spoon, Plate, Disposable plastic tarp, 1 Dozen eggs, Mustard, Mayonnaise, Salt and pepper, Loaf of bread
Day 5	Game Time	Find the Sweets	Large bag sour candies, Large bag identical sweet candies, Resealable plastic snack bags, Marker, Clipboard, Dark-colored paper, Upbeat music
Bonus	Activity Page	Help the Shepherd	1 Copy for each child

Lesson Introduction:

God always triumphs! He wanted a family and for them to be fruitful—BLESSED!

This is a great place to emphasize the difference between Jesus' wonderful plan for our lives and Satan's evil one. Connect the memory verse from last week to give the kids the full picture of what Jesus did for us. He was willing to obey His Father, no matter what He Himself wanted to do (Luke 22:42). Adam and Eve chose to do what *they* wanted to do, so they chose Satan to become their god. Then, they had to live under his rule—the curse. Because of their choice, until Jesus came, their descendants, the rest of mankind, had no choice but to live under the curse. But, Jesus defeated Satan and won the right for us to choose THE BLESSING!

I take every opportunity I can to talk about "The Sweet Life." This is one of the core truths we want the kids to keep in the forefront of their thinking. It's amazing how they grasp this simple truth: God has a plan for them, and when they listen to and obey Him (and His agents in their lives—Mom and Dad), He will give them a life so awesome they can't dream big enough to imagine it (Jeremiah 29:11). I love to see their reactions when they understand this—they get so excited!

Love,

Commander Kellie

Commander Kellie

Lesson Outline:

God only wants the best for His kids. This week, as you teach this lesson, remind your children that God is still in the redeeming business. He had a plan for mankind, way back at the beginning—Jesus—and He has a plan for our lives today!

I. GOD'S FAMILY WAS IN BIG TROUBLE Genesis 3:17

    a. Adam and Eve hid from their heavenly Father.

    b. They had traded God's plan for the devil's plan.

    c. Whenever the devil gets his way, there is secrecy and hiding.

    d. God wants us to run to Him when we're in trouble.

II. GOD HAD A PLAN TO GET HIS CHILDREN BACK

    a. Our heavenly Father was not willing to lose us. John 3:16

    b. No price was too high to get His family back!

    c. He already had a plan to defeat the devil. Genesis 3:15

    d. Jesus was the Lamb slain before the foundation of the world. 1 Peter 1:18-20

III. JESUS BROUGHT US BACK TO THE GARDEN

    a. He rescued us from the curse! Colossians 1:13

    b. Our Savior restored THE BLESSING of God to us. Romans 5:1-2

    c. Satan came to steal, kill and destroy but Jesus came to give life—"The Sweet Life." John 10:10

    d. We have to choose "The Sweet Life"!

Notes:_____

_____

_____

_____

_____

_____

_____

_____

_____

_____

DAY 1: BIBLE LESSON

GOD'S PLAN TO GET HIS CHILDREN BACK

Memory Verse: *The thief's purpose is to steal and kill and destroy. My purpose is to give them a rich and satisfying life.* —John 10:10

Last week, you taught your children about the Fall and Adam and Eve's disobedience to God. This week, they will learn about God's plan for redemption. Reread Genesis 3, and pay special attention to God's plan for getting His children back through Jesus' death and resurrection (verse 15). In addition to the Fall, read what Colossians says about God's redemption through Jesus Christ. Satan came to destroy mankind, but Jesus came to give us The Sweet Life!

Read Genesis 3:1-15:
The Man and Woman Sin

The serpent was the shrewdest of all the wild animals the Lord God had made. One day he asked the woman, "Did God really say you must not eat the fruit from any of the trees in the garden?"

"Of course we may eat fruit from the trees in the garden," the woman replied. "It's only the fruit from the tree in the middle of the garden that we are not allowed to eat. God said, 'You must not eat it or even touch it; if you do, you will die.'"

"You won't die!" the serpent replied to the woman. "God knows that your eyes will be opened as soon as you eat it, and you will be like God, knowing both good and evil."

The woman was convinced. She saw that the tree was beautiful and its fruit looked delicious, and she wanted the wisdom it would give her. So she took some of the fruit and ate it. Then she gave some to her husband, who was with her, and he ate it, too. At that moment their eyes were opened, and they suddenly felt shame at their nakedness. So they sewed fig leaves together to cover themselves.

When the cool evening breezes were blowing, the man and his wife heard the Lord God walking about in the garden. So they hid from the Lord God among the trees. Then the Lord God called to the man, "Where are you?"

He replied, "I heard You walking in the garden, so I hid. I was afraid because I was naked."

"Who told you that you were naked?" the Lord God asked. "Have you eaten from the tree whose fruit I commanded you not to eat?"

The man replied, "It was the woman You gave me who gave me the fruit, and I ate it."

Then the Lord God asked the woman, "What have you done?"

"The serpent deceived me," she replied. "That's why I ate it."

Then the Lord God said to the serpent, "Because you have done this, you are cursed more than all animals, domestic and wild. You will crawl on your belly, groveling in the dust as long as you live. <u>And I will cause hostility between you and the woman, and between your offspring and her offspring. He will strike your head, and you will strike his heel.</u>"

Read Colossians 1:13-20:

<u>For he has rescued us from the kingdom of darkness and transferred us into the Kingdom of his dear Son, who purchased our freedom and forgave our sins.</u> Christ is the visible image of the invisible God. He existed before anything was created and is supreme over all creation, for through him God created everything in the heavenly realms and on earth. He made the things we can see and the things we can't see—such as thrones, kingdoms, rulers, and authorities in the unseen world. Everything was created through him and for him. He existed before anything else, and he holds all creation together. Christ is also the head of the church, which is his body. He is the beginning, supreme over all who rise from the dead. So he is first in everything. For God in all his fullness was pleased to live in Christ, and <u>through him God reconciled everything to himself. He made peace with everything in heaven and on earth by means of Christ's blood on the cross.</u>

Discussion Questions:

1. **What did God mean when He said, "I will cause hostility between you and the woman, and between your offspring and her offspring. He will strike your head, and you will strike his heel"?**
   God was telling Satan that Jesus was coming. Satan would attack Jesus, but Jesus would win.

2. **Who is Jesus?**
   Jesus is God's Son and the only person to live a perfect life, without sin. According to Colossians 1, He is:

   - God's presence in the earth
   - The Creator of everything
   - The One who holds everything together
   - The Head of the Church
   - Supreme over all Creation
   - First in everything
   - The One who reconciled Creation to God

3. **What did His death mean for us?**
   Through Jesus' death and resurrection, we are forgiven of our sins and no longer live under the curse. Through Him, we have freedom, eternal life and access to THE BLESSING. Because of what Jesus did for us, we will one day live in heaven with God.

4. **What does it mean for Jesus to be first in everything? What does it mean to have Him be first in our lives?**
   Jesus is the Head, or leader, of Creation. He holds it all together. He should be supreme, or first, in our lives too. Everything we do should be done for Him and with Him in mind.

Variation No. 1: Video

Bring the story of the Fall and God's promise of redemption to life through an animated video. Your local library is a good resource for finding children's videos on well-known Bible stories.

Variation No. 2: Journaling

Older children can journal what it means for them to have freedom through Jesus Christ. What does their salvation mean to them?

Variation No. 3: Bible Study

Older children will benefit from a more in-depth Bible study on God's redemptive plan for mankind. Here are a few verses to get them started: John 3:16; 1 Peter 1:18-20; Romans 5:1-2; John 10:10.

Notes: _____

_____

_____

_____

_____

_____

_____

_____

_____

_____

_____

_____

_____

_____

_____

_____

_____

_____

_____

_____

_____

_____

_____

_____

DAY 2: READ-ALOUD

BEST-CASE SCENARIO: "RISE TO THE TOP"

Suggested Time: 15 minutes

Memory Verse: The thief's purpose is to steal and kill and destroy. My purpose is to give them a rich and satisfying life. —John 10:10

Lesson Instructions:

Welcome to Best-Case Scenario, where you'll see ordinary Christian kids in everyday situations.

"What's so exciting about that?" you may ask.

Well, stick with it. In just a moment, you'll see an everyday challenge turn into a Best-Case Scenario. In other words, the best possible outcome of a normal situation.

First, meet John Mark. He is 11 years old. His hobbies include video games, paper football and spitting long distances. His favorite phrase is, "Church it up!"

John Mark's neighbor Nick is 15 years old. His hobbies include all-night video game rallies, skateboarding and sleeping. His favorite phrase is, "Whoa!"

Can John Mark convince the skating video-head Nick that Jesus is the One and only defeater of every level of hell? Will Nick believe that Jesus paid the highest price to save him? Let's find out.

John Mark is sitting at his kitchen table practicing his paper football skills when Nick's face peers through his backdoor window. John Mark motions to him. "Come in," he says. "Perfect timing. Don't move."

Nick enters, holding a few video games in his hand, and John Mark launches the paper football at him.

"Yo, what's happenin'?" Nick asks.

"Yo, not much. Just practicing my paper-football skills," John Mark says.

"Righteous. I just came over to bring back your 'Rise to the Top' game. And, I also brought you something else, just for being such a cool dude who let me borrow your games." Nick hands John Mark a new game. "Check it out—'Bottom Feeder From Hell 5.' There's like these creepy dudes who spray green poison puke at you—it rocks."

"Uh, that's really nice of you. I don't think I'll borrow it, though." John Mark hands the game back. "But speaking of hell, I know a lot about it."

"You do?" Nick asks with wide eyes.

"Yeah, my best friend has actually beaten every hell game out there," John Mark says simply.

"Right on! But whoa, dude. How is that even like totally possible? There are so many hell games," Nick says excitedly, and punches John Mark in the arm.

"Well, He's really been there."

"No way!"

"Way," John Mark nods. "He actually went to hell and lived to tell about it."

"Whoa."

John Mark continues, "Whoa is right. He did all that so you could be a part of His family."

"Dude, I always wanted to be adopted!"

"His name is Jesus, God's Son, and He came so you could live a great life—He's got awesome plans for you," John Mark said.

"I always wanted to skate in the X-Games. Would you ask Him if that's in the plan?" Nick asks.

"No, but you can."

"Whoa. I don't know, dude. I'm not like the pope. Praying is not really my kind of thing."

"It's easy. If you want, I can help you pray right now. All you have to do is repeat after me."

"Right on." Nick takes John Mark's hand and they bow their heads to pray.

There you have it: a Best-Case Scenario. Instead of watching and being scared by "Bottom Feeder From Hell 5," John Mark uses it to talk about Jesus, the ultimate "Rise to the Top" example. Nick commits his life to God and joins a Christian skater club training for the X-Games, and to show his thanks, trades in "Bottom Feeder From Hell 5" for "Grand-Slam Baseball" as a gift to John Mark.

Talk about a Best-Case Scenario. It just doesn't get much better than that!

Discussion Questions:

Use these questions as conversation starters. Enjoy this time of heart-to-heart conversation with your children.

1. **How did John Mark share Jesus with Nick? Did he speak to him in a way Nick could understand?**

2. **Do you have a friend who needs to hear about Jesus?**

3. **Have you ever shared Jesus with him/her? What happened?**

4. **Parents, discuss a time when you shared Jesus with someone. What did you think? What did you feel? What did you say? Seize this opportunity to teach your children about sharing Jesus with their friends and family.**

Notes: _____

_____

_____

_____

_____

_____

_____

_____

DAY 3: GIVING LESSON

WHO'S INVITED?

Suggested Time: 10 minutes

Offering Scripture: Then he turned to his host. "When you put on a luncheon or a banquet," he said, "don't invite your friends, brothers, relatives, and rich neighbors. For they will invite you back, and that will be your only reward. Instead, invite the poor, the crippled, the lame, and the blind. Then at the resurrection of the righteous, God will reward you for inviting those who could not repay you." —Luke 14:12-14

Supplies: ☐ A birthday cake and candles

Lesson Instructions:

Mmmmm, birthday cake!

Who wants to share a little cake with me?

I have so much fun at birthday parties, and you know, the more friends at the party, the better! But, did you know there are kids who don't get invited to parties very often? Maybe they don't fit in with the rest of the kids very well. They're the ones no one wants to play with or invite to their house. You could maybe call them the "outsiders."

Did you know Jesus had something to say to us about the "outsiders"? Let me read what the Bible says: "Then he turned to his host. 'When you put on a luncheon or a banquet,' he said, 'don't invite your friends, brothers, relatives, and rich neighbors. For they will invite you back, and that will be your only reward. Instead, invite the poor, the crippled, the lame, and the blind. Then at the resurrection of the righteous, God will reward you for inviting those who could not repay you.'"

Jesus was describing people who were different. He loved the "outsiders," the ones who didn't seem to fit in. When you invite the friendless to your birthday party, or play with them when no one else will, you are acting like Jesus. And, Jesus never leaves people on the outside. He came to bring everyone to the "inside," close to Him and His family! Listen to this: Jesus said when you do this you will be a blessing and you will be blessed, too!

Variation:

Consider reaching out to a new friend or someone who doesn't have many friends. Invite them to your home for a play date or a park date. Let this be an opportunity to apply what your child has learned. Would you like to invite someone over today who isn't very popular or maybe we don't play with very often? Or, maybe there's a new kid we haven't spent time with yet. Maybe we could invite him or her to meet us at the park for some fun. We could even share our birthday cake with our new friend!

Notes: _____

_____

_____

_____

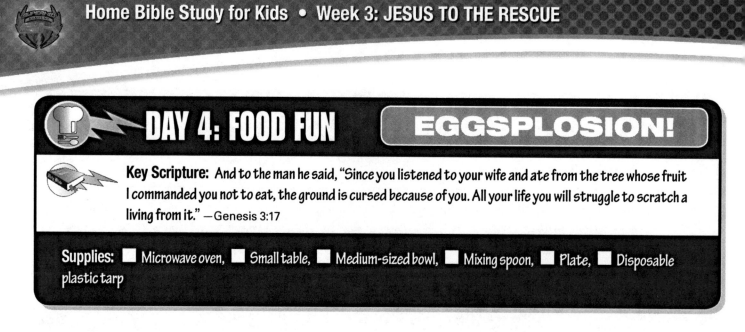

DAY 4: FOOD FUN — EGGSPLOSION!

Key Scripture: And to the man he said, "Since you listened to your wife and ate from the tree whose fruit I commanded you not to eat, the ground is cursed because of you. All your life you will struggle to scratch a living from it." —Genesis 3:17

Supplies: ☐ Microwave oven, ☐ Small table, ☐ Medium-sized bowl, ☐ Mixing spoon, ☐ Plate, ☐ Disposable plastic tarp

Prior to Lesson:

Prep the area prior to your time together, so when you put down the tarp you are not tipping the kids off to the possibility of a mess. The element of surprise in this lesson will make a big impact—you will be exploding an egg in the microwave oven. (Note: This took 56 seconds on the high setting in our microwave oven.)

Be sure to stand to the side of the oven because the explosion will force the door open. It makes quite an impressive pop— a little messy, but worth the effort. There is no smoke or burnt smell, just small pieces of egg here and there! A little cleanup tip: Place a cup of water in the microwave oven. Heat for 2-3 minutes and let stand for a few more minutes. The steam will loosen the egg particles. (Make sure there is plenty of space to keep your microwave a safe distance from your group.)

Lesson Instructions:

How many of you have had an egg-salad sandwich?

They're very yummy and easy to make, so I thought I'd teach you how to make egg salad today. I have all my ingredients: eggs, mayonnaise, mustard (I like lots of mustard in mine), salt and pepper. There's just one little problem though, the recipe said I was supposed to boil the eggs first, but I ran out of time, so I didn't get that part done before we started today.

But, I had this thought: I'll just cook them in the microwave. It'll be faster, anyway. *(Place a whole, uncooked egg, still in the shell, in the center of the microwave oven and set it for 1 1/2 minutes; be sure and stand to the side and continue talking as the egg cooks.)* Well, the egg should be ready any time now…. *(Continue with small talk until the egg explodes.)*

Whoa! What happened here? I guess my idea of putting eggs in the microwave wasn't so good. Learn from my mistake and never put an egg that's still in the shell in the microwave!

This reminds me of a couple of people in the Bible who didn't do things the right way, either. Yes, I'm talking about Adam and Eve. Instead of doing what God had told them, they had their own idea. They believed the lies of the devil and disobeyed God. Just like my idea to microwave this egg caused a big explosion and made a big mess, so did Adam and Eve's idea to follow the devil. My mess can be cleaned up with just a little soap and water, but Adam and Eve's mess could be cleaned up only one way—by the blood of Jesus. I am so thankful that Jesus was willing to clean up Adam and Eve's mess. How about you?

Egg-salad sandwich recipe:

Ingredients: ☐ 1 Dozen eggs, ☐ Mustard, ☐ Mayonnaise, ☐ Salt and pepper, ☐ Loaf of bread

1. Cover remaining eggs with cold water
2. Boil 1 minute.
3. Cool for 13 minutes.
4. Then drain and peel. You will have perfect hard-boiled eggs!
5. Chop eggs and add mustard, mayo, salt and pepper to taste

While the kids are "building" their sandwiches, adding pickles and lettuce, you can discuss how the timing was important! This can segue into a great discussion on different issues that your kids are facing. What is hard to wait for? Why don't we like to wait? Was it worth the wait?

Notes: _____

_____

_____

_____

_____

_____

_____

_____

_____

_____

_____

_____

_____

_____

_____

_____

_____

_____

_____

DAY 5: GAME TIME — FIND THE SWEETS

Suggested Time: 5-10 minutes

Memory Verse: The thief's purpose is to steal and kill and destroy. My purpose is to give them a rich and satisfying life. —John 10:10

Supplies: ☐ Large bag of sour candies, ☐ Large bag of identical sweet candies, ☐ Resealable plastic snack bags for the candy, ☐ Marker (to label bags), ☐ Clipboard with "game-round" descriptions (rounds listed at bottom of outline), ☐ Dark-colored paper, ☐ Upbeat music to play during the game

Prior to Game:

Place the "game-round" description paper on a clipboard, covered by dark-colored paper, so the kids cannot see the answers. Prepare two of the resealable snack bags with 15 mixed sweet and sour candies in each for each round of play. Label the two bags with the game-round number. See "Round" description below for numbers. Be sure to place the same amount of candy in both candy bags.

Game Instructions:

Does anyone like sweets? How about candy?

That's great—because this game is all about finding sweets. In each bag there are 15 candies. Some are sweet and some are sour. I need you to tell me how many sweet candies are in each snack bag.

And what is the best way to figure that out? Eat them!

- Choose two players.
- Give each player a Round No. 1 bag of candy.
- On "go," have players eat the candy, keeping track silently of how many sweet ones they find. Once both players have finished eating their candies, have them whisper their answer to you. Tell the others playing the game what their answers are before announcing the winner. Play three to six rounds, depending on your preference and time availability.

Game Goal:

During the excitement of a game, it can be difficult to concentrate. Be sure to block out distractions and not lose count!

Final Word:

All those candies looked sweet—but some were really sour. Isn't it good to know that the life God wants for us is ALWAYS sweet and never sour? What are some of the things that make life "sweet"? What are some that make it "sour"? With Jesus it really is "The Sweet Life!"

Round No. 1	Round No. 2	Round No. 3	Round No. 4	Round No. 5	Round No. 6
Sweet 3 Sour 12	Sweet 8 Sour 7	Sweet 5 Sour 10	Sweet 7 Sour 8	Sweet 9 Sour 6	Sweet 4 Sour 11

Notes: _____

_____

_____

_____

_____

_____

_____

_____

_____

_____

_____

_____

_____

_____

_____

_____

_____

_____

_____

_____

_____

_____

_____

_____

_____

ACTIVITY PAGE — HELP THE SHEPHERD

Memory Verse: The thief's purpose is to steal and kill and destroy. My purpose is to give them a rich and satisfying life. —John 10:10

When Adam and Eve sinned, God didn't give up on mankind. He had a plan to redeem His people through His Son, Jesus. He helped them return to safety.

In this game, you can help the shepherd find his lost sheep and return it to safety.

In this word search, help the shepherd find the lost words. The first one is done for you.

1. SHEEP
2. SHEPHERD
3. PASTURE
4. SATISFYING
5. LIFE
6. THIEF
7. STEAL
8. WOOL
9. SHEEPFOLD
10. RICH
11. SAFETY
12. PURPOSE

```
Q M F D P U R P O S E A W M F K P B F Q P E
G N G S L E X N G A L W O N G A L S G A F P
N B H Z H I C B H Z K E O B H Z K H H I K A
I V J X M H D V J X M R L V J X M E L X M S
Y C K D S T E A L D N T T C K D N E K D N T
F X L E J Y V H L E J Y Y X L E J P L E J U
S Z P F D R E H P E H S U Z P V I F P V I R
I A O E O I G A O R O S A F E T Y O O F O E
T S I I U O H C I R D O O S I R U L I R U O
A D U H H P N D U B H P P D U B H D U B H P
S F Y T B A J S H E E P A F Y G B A Y G B A
```

WEEK 4: HONOR GOD

 **Memory Verse:** But I will honor those who honor me, and I will despise those who think lightly of me.—1 Samuel 2:30b

WEEK 4: SNAPSHOT — HONOR GOD

DAY	TYPE OF LESSON	LESSON TITLE	SUPPLIES
Day 1	Bible Lesson	The Lord Rejects Saul	None
Day 2	Object Lesson	Easy Ways	Dirty and wrinkled shirt, Clean and neat shirt on a hanger, 1 Severely beaten-up Bible, 1 Written-in and underlined but well-treated Bible, Bag (to place Bibles in), Candy or gum
Day 3	Giving Lesson	Just Between Us	4" x 6" Notecards , Small envelopes, Pencils or pens
Day 4	Food Fun	Put God on Top	Small table, Large clear glass, Hand-held blender or eggbeater, Long-handled spoon, Quart-sized resealable food-storage bag, Hard plastic hammer or mallet, Cutting board, Drinking straw, 12-16 Ounces of cold milk, Chocolate syrup, Malted milk powder, Secret ingredient: 2-3 Tablespoons of whipped dessert topping powder (usually found on grocery aisle with pudding mixes), 1 Pressurized can of whipped cream, 1 Box of malted milk balls
Day 5	Game Time	Tic-Tac-Treat	9 Lunchboxes or similar-sized containers, Lunch-style "treats" to place in each box (string cheese, small candies, fruit pies, cupcakes, etc.), Clipboard, Questions from previous week's teaching, Background game music, Sticky-backed hook and loop fastener (or tape), 5 Large laminated X's and 5 large laminated O's (See pages 72 and 73 for templates.)
Bonus	Activity Page	Honor Word Search	1 Copy for each child

Lesson Introduction:

The story of Saul and the bleating sheep is an excellent way to illustrate a lack of honor. Try to tell the story very dramatically. Get it in your heart as you read it several times in your own study time. Saul didn't honor God as his Commander or his hope of victory. People fail in life for the same reason. Ecclesiastes 12:13 AMP says that the fear (respect, honor) of the Lord and keeping His Word will adjust any circumstance in our own lives. Many people think of Jesus as their Lord, but they don't listen to or obey Him. Like Saul (1 Samuel 15:13), they are fooling themselves, honoring their own ideas above His.

Jesus is our greatest example of honoring His Father every day. This habitual obedience prepared Him to face His greatest challenge. When He had to make the hardest choice of His life, He chose to honor what the Father wanted. When our Superkids live like Jesus, and receive His will and instructions with honor, their lives will produce "The Sweet Life" that Jesus paid for (Colossians 1:10; Galatians 6:8-9)!

Love,

Commander Kellie

Commander Kellie

Lesson Outline:

Through Jesus, your children have access to The Sweet Life. They can live in THE BLESSING, and for them to fully enjoy all that God has for them, they must obey and honor Him. Use the next few weeks to focus on what honor is and how to live a life of honor—to God, to you as their parents, and to the Holy Spirit.

I. WE HONOR GOD BY LIVING LIFE AS HE DIRECTS

a. *Honor:* "to hold in highest respect, regard, esteem."

b. There are three steps to show honor to God:

   1. <u>Listen</u> — Put His words first place in your life.
      Jeremiah 13:11 NIV — They wouldn't listen = no honor.

   2. <u>Submit</u> — Decide that His way is always the right way.
      Proverbs 3:5-7 — Trust His wisdom, not your own.

   3. <u>Obey</u> — Quickly, without having to think about it.
      Luke 6:46 — You aren't letting Him be your Lord when you don't obey.

II. SAUL DID NOT HONOR GOD 1 Samuel 15

a. Saul didn't listen to God's instructions. Verses 2-3

b. Saul didn't submit—he had a better idea. Verse 9

c. Saul didn't obey—he dishonored God. Verses 10-23

d. He was afraid of what people thought. Verse 24

III. JESUS LIVED HIS LIFE TO HONOR GOD

a. Jesus always listened to His Father. John 8:28

b. Jesus was always submitted to His Father. John 8:29

c. Jesus always obeyed His Father. Mark 14:36

Notes:_____

_____

_____

_____

_____

_____

_____

_____

DAY 1: BIBLE LESSON — THE LORD REJECTS SAUL

Memory Verse: But I will honor those who honor me, and I will despise those who think lightly of me.
—1 Samuel 2:30b

This week begins our series about honor. This is such an important topic because a successful Christian life begins with honoring our heavenly Father. Through honor—and obedience—to Him and His Word, we are able to live The Sweet Life and walk in THE BLESSING.

As you teach your children this week, help them understand that honoring and obeying the Lord go hand in hand— they cannot do one without the other. Thankfully, as they study, meditate on and obey the Word, the Holy Spirit will help them accomplish all that God desires.

Read 1 Samuel 15:
Saul Destroys the Amalekites

One day Samuel said to Saul, "It was the Lord who told me to anoint you as king of his people, Israel. Now listen to this message from the Lord! This is what the Lord of Heaven's Armies has declared: I have decided to settle accounts with the nation of Amalek for opposing Israel when they came from Egypt. Now go and completely destroy the entire Amalekite nation—men, women, children, babies, cattle, sheep, goats, camels, and donkeys."

So Saul mobilized his army at Telaim. There were 200,000 soldiers from Israel and 10,000 men from Judah. Then Saul and his army went to a town of the Amalekites and lay in wait in the valley. Saul sent this warning to the Kenites: "Move away from where the Amalekites live, or you will die with them. For you showed kindness to all the people of Israel when they came up from Egypt." So the Kenites packed up and left.

Then Saul slaughtered the Amalekites from Havilah all the way to Shur, east of Egypt. He captured Agag, the Amalekite king, but completely destroyed everyone else. Saul and his men spared Agag's life and kept the best of the sheep and goats, the cattle, the fat calves, and the lambs—everything, in fact, that appealed to them. They destroyed only what was worthless or of poor quality.

The Lord Rejects Saul

Then the Lord said to Samuel, "I am sorry that I ever made Saul king, for he has not been loyal to me and has refused to obey my command." Samuel was so deeply moved when he heard this that he cried out to the Lord all night.

Early the next morning Samuel went to find Saul. Someone told him, "Saul went to the town of Carmel to set up a monument to himself; then he went on to Gilgal."

When Samuel finally found him, Saul greeted him cheerfully. "May the Lord bless you," he said. "I have carried out the Lord's command!"

"Then what is all the bleating of sheep and goats and the lowing of cattle I hear?" Samuel demanded.

"It's true that the army spared the best of the sheep, goats, and cattle," Saul admitted. "But they are going to sacrifice them to the Lord your God. We have destroyed everything else."

Then Samuel said to Saul, "Stop! Listen to what the Lord told me last night!"

"What did he tell you?" Saul asked.

And Samuel told him, "Although you may think little of yourself, are you not the leader of the tribes of Israel? The Lord has anointed you king of Israel. And the Lord sent you on a mission and told you, 'Go and completely destroy the sinners, the Amalekites, until they are all dead.' Why haven't you obeyed the Lord? Why did you rush for the plunder and do what was evil in the Lord's sight?"

"But I did obey the Lord," Saul insisted. "I carried out the mission he gave me. I brought back King Agag, but I destroyed everyone else. Then my troops brought in the best of the sheep, goats, cattle, and plunder to sacrifice to the Lord your God in Gilgal."

But Samuel replied, "What is more pleasing to the Lord: your burnt offerings and sacrifices or your obedience to his voice? Listen! Obedience is better than sacrifice, and submission is better than offering the fat of rams. Rebellion is as sinful as witchcraft, and stubbornness as bad as worshiping idols. So because you have rejected the command of the Lord, he has rejected you as king."

Saul Pleads for Forgiveness

Then Saul admitted to Samuel, "Yes, I have sinned. I have disobeyed your instructions and the Lord's command, for I was afraid of the people and did what they demanded. But now, please forgive my sin and come back with me so that I may worship the Lord."

But Samuel replied, "I will not go back with you! Since you have rejected the Lord's command, he has rejected you as king of Israel."

As Samuel turned to go, Saul tried to hold him back and tore the hem of his robe. And Samuel said to him, "The Lord has torn the kingdom of Israel from you today and has given it to someone else—one who is better than you. And he who is the Glory of Israel will not lie, nor will he change his mind, for he is not human that he should change his mind!"

Then Saul pleaded again, "I know I have sinned. But please, at least honor me before the elders of my people and before Israel by coming back with me so that I may worship the Lord your God." So Samuel finally agreed and went back with him, and Saul worshiped the Lord.

Samuel Executes King Agag

Then Samuel said, "Bring King Agag to me." Agag arrived full of hope, for he thought, "Surely the worst is over, and I have been spared!" But Samuel said, "As your sword has killed the sons of many mothers, now your mother will be childless." And Samuel cut Agag to pieces before the Lord at Gilgal.

Then Samuel went home to Ramah, and Saul returned to his house at Gibeah of Saul. Samuel never went to meet with Saul again, but he mourned constantly for him. And the Lord was sorry he had ever made Saul king of Israel.

Discussion Questions:

1. **Name three things that happened in this passage.**
   Answers will vary, but use this time of discussion to make sure your children understand the passage.

2. **What did God instruct Saul to do?**
   God told Saul to destroy everything in the Amalekite nation—people and animals.

3. **What did Saul do instead?**

He spared King Agag and the best of the animals. He only destroyed what was worthless and kept the best for himself and his soldiers.

4. **Why did Saul disobey God? What was the real reason for his disobedience?**
He cared more about pleasing his people than about obeying God. The people wanted to salvage the best animals and goods from the Amalekites instead of destroying them.

5. **What was the result of this disobedience?**
God rejected him and regretted making him king of Israel.

6. **Saul tried to justify his actions by saying that he planned to sacrifice the animals and goods that he had kept to the Lord. How did Samuel respond to that statement?**
He said, "Obedience is better than sacrifice, and submission is better than offering the fat of rams" (verse 22).

7. **What did Samuel mean by that?**
Obedience is more important than going through a ritual or ceremony—even a good one. If Saul had truly wanted to honor the Lord, he would have obeyed Him.

8. **How can we obey God?**
We can obey Him by honoring:

- His Word

- The authority He places in our lives

- His Holy Spirit

9. **How are obeying God and honoring God alike?**
It is impossible to honor God without obeying Him and His Word.

Variation: Personal Experience

Your children can learn a lot about walking with the Lord from your example. Share about a time when you obeyed the Lord—even when it was difficult—and what the result of that obedience was. You may even share a time when you *didn't* obey the Lord and how that disobedience affected you. Let this be a time of open and honest communication, of both talking and listening. Let the Holy Spirit lead you in the best way to teach your children His truth.

Notes: _____

_____

_____

_____

_____

_____

_____

_____

_____

_____

_____

DAY 2: OBJECT LESSON — EASY WAYS

Suggested Time: *10 minutes*

Memory Verse: *But I will honor those who honor me, and I will despise those who think lightly of me.*—1 Samuel 2:30b

Supplies: ☐ Dirty and wrinkled shirt, ☐ Clean and neat shirt on a hanger, ☐ 1 Severely beaten-up Bible (Lost and Found at your church can sometimes provide one to borrow), ☐ 1 Written-in and underlined but well-treated Bible, ☐ Bag (to place Bibles in), ☐ Candy or gum

Lesson Instructions:

For the next few weeks, we're going to talk about honor.

Can you tell me what honor means? *(Allow for answers.)*

Honor means "to respect." When you respect someone, you want to please them and treat them well.

Who do you think is the most important person we can ever honor and respect?

Our heavenly Father—that's right! There is no one more important to honor than God. So today, we're going to learn how to honor God. In fact, I'm going to give you three easy ways you can show God honor, but I need your help to demonstrate it.

1. <u>We can honor God by pleasing Him.</u>

Before you go to church, what do you have to change?

Your clothes, right? So you look around and see your favorite shirt on the floor. *(Wad up the dirty shirt and throw it on the floor. Pick it up.)* It's a little bit wrinkled and has a couple of spots. Those are chocolate stains from that birthday party last week! Oh well, it's just church. No big deal, OR you could wear this other shirt that's hanging up. *(Have the clean, hanging shirt nearby.)* It's neat and clean, although it's not your favorite—it sure does look a lot nicer.

Which choice do you think would show God more honor and be pleasing to Him?

(Have your child put on the shirt they think is the honor choice.)

EASY!

2. <u>We can honor God by honoring His Word.</u>

You'll have no problem figuring this one out. Now that you've gotten dressed, you need to bring something to church.

What is it? *(Take out two Bibles from the bag.)*

Your Bible! There are two Bibles to choose from. This Bible has been studied and written in, but it still looks really nice. Somebody who really loves God's Word has had this Bible. There are no torn pages or bent corners. Let's look at the other one. Wow! Somebody has been really mean to this Bible. It's so beaten up. And they've written cartoons all over it. I think they've even played tic-tac-toe inside!

Which Bible do you think would show more honor to God?

(Have your child pick the Bible they think is the honor choice.)

EASY!

3. We can honor God by caring more about Him than about what our friends think.

So, you've gotten dressed, brought your Bible, and you're finally at church. Now it's time for one of your favorite things, praise and worship. Woohoo!

(Have your child raise their hands, then nudge them and pull out the candy.)

But, just when you start to worship God, one of your friends nudges you. They have a piece of candy to give you. You really want to focus on God right now, but you also don't want to make your friend mad.

Should you take the candy and eat it, or politely shake your head no, then close your eyes to block out the distraction? What do you think would honor God more?

(Have your child tell you which action would be the honor choice.)

EASY, AGAIN!

See, honoring God and pleasing Him isn't hard at all! I'll review them one last time:

1. Honor God by pleasing Him, like being considerate and dressing nice for Him.

2. Honor God by respecting His Word; that means studying and taking care of your Bible!

3. Honor God by caring more about Him than about what your friends think.

If you can remember these three easy ways to honor God, you will show Him how much you love Him. Of course, He is always super-proud to be your Dad!

Notes: _____

_____

_____

_____

_____

_____

_____

_____

_____

_____

_____

_____

_____

_____

DAY 3: GIVING LESSON — JUST BETWEEN US

Suggested Time: *10 minutes*

Offering Scripture: *Don't worry about anything; instead, pray about everything. Tell God what you need, and thank him for all he has done.* —Philippians 4:6

Supplies: ☐ *4"x 6" Notecards*, ☐ *Small envelopes*, ☐ *Pencils or pens*

Lesson Instructions:

Kids, I'd like to talk to you about a subject every young person is interested in—growing up. I'm sure you have dreamed of the day you could drive a car. Am I right?

Or, maybe you've thought about being old enough to get a job so you could have more money to spend on things you'd like to have. It's pretty normal for kids to dream about being a teenager or even a grown-up.

Well, I don't know if you have thought about this, but as you learn more about God and your spirit man, the Holy Spirit will start to teach you how to trust God for things on your own. Your spirit is the real you that the Bible calls your "heart"!

I have a great idea I want to try out, but I'll need your help.

(Have each family member participate. Wait until you have explained the entire process before handing out the supplies. Be ready to have someone assist the smaller children with writing if needed.)

Before we get started, I want to read a verse to you. Philippians 4:6 says, "Don't worry about anything; instead, pray about everything." When you're a kid, who do you usually talk to when there is something you need? Mom and Dad, right? Now, here's your challenge: This scripture is saying that we should pray and let God know our concerns. So, instead of always asking your parents to get you everything you need, why not ask God and let it be between just you and Him? That doesn't mean it's wrong to talk to your dad (or mom) and me, in fact you need to be very open with us. But it's good to practice depending on God.

This is what I want you to do; write a note to the Lord letting Him know what you need, and then put it in your envelope and seal it up. This is going to be between just you and God. Don't tell others about what you wrote, and don't be concerned—it's now God's job to take care of whatever you put on your paper. Now, this will be the best part: When God answers the prayer you wrote down, bring your envelope to me. If you want, we can open it right here and celebrate what God did.

Check this out—did you realize that you just grew up a little bit when you decided to pray and trust God for yourself?

Notes: _____

_____

_____

_____

_____

_____

DAY 4: FOOD FUN

PUT GOD ON TOP

Suggested Time: 10 minutes

Key Scripture: For you gladly honor each other, but you don't care about the honor that comes from the one who alone is God.—John 5:44

Teacher Tip: In this recipe, you have a secret ingredient! Remove the whipped dessert topping packet from the box and label it "Secret Ingredient" with a felt-tip marker. The whipped dessert topping will make your milk thick and frothy.

Recipe:

Ingredients: ☐ 12-16 Ounces of cold milk, ☐ Chocolate syrup, ☐ Malted milk powder, ☐ Secret ingredient: 2-3 Tablespoons of whipped dessert topping powder (usually found on grocery aisle with pudding mixes), ☐ 1 Pressurized can of whipped cream, ☐ 1 Box of malted milk balls

1. Start by pouring cold milk into glass—be sure to leave plenty of room to add syrup, malted milk powder and the secret ingredient. Mix with the blender. (Could also be mixed in a blender and poured into the glass after blending.)

2. Add chocolate syrup and malted milk powder, to taste. Don't hold back on the chocolate syrup—kids like their milk pretty chocolaty!

3. Mix with hand-held blender until well-blended.

4. While mixing your milk, have an assistant place about half the box of malted milk balls in the food-storage bag and seal tightly. Place bag on the cutting board and, using the hammer or mallet, crush the candy into big chunks.

5. Add the whipped dessert topping powder to milk and mix until frothy.

6. Finish off your treat with whipped cream and malted milk ball pieces on top!

Supplies: ☐ Small table, ☐ Large, clear glass, ☐ Hand-held blender or eggbeater, ☐ Long-handled spoon, ☐ Quart-sized resealable food-storage bag, ☐ Hard, plastic hammer or mallet, ☐ Cutting board (for hammer base), ☐ Drinking straw, ☐ Chocolate milk ingredients

Lesson Instructions:

Kids, today we're making a yummy treat, but before we get started, can you help me? I know you'll be good with a hammer!

(Choose an older child since they will be using a somewhat-heavy tool.)

You know how to make a glass of chocolate milk, don't you?

Well, today we are making a fancy version of chocolate milk because instead of just putting in chocolate syrup, we'll be adding some malted milk powder (that's the stuff they use when they make malted milk balls) and a secret ingredient that will make our milk a little frothy, kind of like whipped cream. Let's get started!

(Proceed by following the recipe instructions, but stop after completing step 4.)

Now for the secret ingredient! (Make a big deal out of step 5.)

Kids, we have been learning a lot about honoring God. Did you know that just like we had a secret ingredient in our chocolate milk, there is a secret ingredient to honoring God? That's right—the secret ingredient is obeying His Word. Just think about it—when we do what God says, we are automatically honoring Him. It just goes together!

We've had a lot of fun making this recipe but did you notice that we're not quite done? Yes, the last part may just be the yummiest of all—it's the ingredients that go on top.

(Finish off the recipe by completing step 6.)

The whipped cream and malted milk balls might just be the best part of the whole recipe—it could be the most delicious, above all the rest. That reminds me of something Jesus said in John 5:44. He told us that we should honor God above all other people. It's kind of like this whipped cream being on the top—it really wouldn't work well to put it in the bottom of the glass, would it? No, it always goes on top of desserts. And, that reminds us of what Jesus was telling us. Make sure you always keep God at the very top of the list of those you honor!

Notes: _____

_____

_____

_____

_____

_____

_____

_____

_____

_____

_____

_____

_____

_____

_____

_____

_____

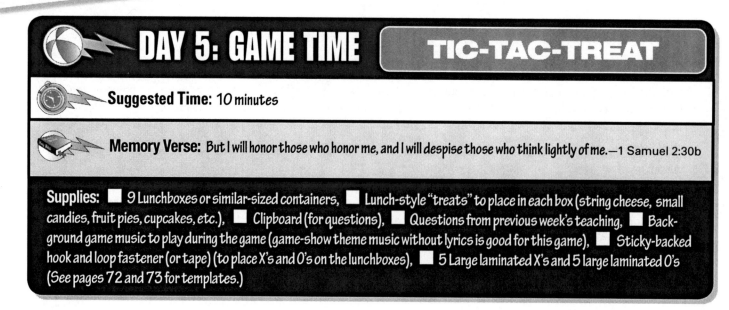

DAY 5: GAME TIME — TIC-TAC-TREAT

Suggested Time: 10 minutes

Memory Verse: But I will honor those who honor me, and I will despise those who think lightly of me.—1 Samuel 2:30b

Supplies: ■ 9 Lunchboxes or similar-sized containers, ■ Lunch-style "treats" to place in each box (string cheese, small candies, fruit pies, cupcakes, etc.), ■ Clipboard (for questions), ■ Questions from previous week's teaching, ■ Background game music to play during the game (game-show theme music without lyrics is good for this game), ■ Sticky-backed hook and loop fastener (or tape) (to place X's and O's on the lunchboxes), ■ 5 Large laminated X's and 5 large laminated O's (See pages 72 and 73 for templates.)

Variation No. 1: Original Questions

Questions and answers have been provided, but if you would like to write your own questions, there is a question template provided.

Variation No. 2: Dress Up

Make it a game-show night complete with a host/assistant costumes—glitzy jackets, sunglasses, dress, etc.

Variation No. 3: Applause

Have someone hold up an applause sign at appropriate moments, like a TV game show.

Prior to Game:

This is a "game series" that corresponds with the teaching series. Because of this, the initial preparation may take a little more effort, but it's a favorite! Let your Superkids know that you will be playing this game the next few weeks of your Honor teaching series, and use questions from the week before to play Tic-Tac-Treat. Watch how your group purposely pays attention!

1. On the back of each lunchbox, place two pieces of sticky-backed hook and loop fastener. You will want to place them in a good position to hold your laminated X or O.

2. Copy five X's and five O's onto a brightly colored paper (yellow is good). We recommend using the same color for all your X's and O's, in case some Superkids catch a glimpse of the color behind the lunchbox. Super-smart Cadets will figure out different colors.

3. Laminate the X's and O's so they will not tear when being switched from box to box on following weeks. (See pages 72 and 73 for templates.)

4. Place the corresponding pieces of sticky-backed fastener on your laminated X's and O's.

5. With sticky fastener, place an X or O to each lunchbox. You will have one X or one O left over. If you used more X's than O's, for instance, the next week you will want to do the opposite.

6. Place a treat in each lunchbox.

7. Place the lunchboxes at the front of the room, with the X's and O's facing away from the Superkids.

8. Place review questions on the clipboard. (Write your own or use the ones provided.)

Game Instructions:

- Begin the game-show music immediately. This game is all about presentation. To kick it up a notch, use a game-show assistant to turn your lunchboxes around (like a glamorous game-show assistant would, with dramatic hand-waving.) We also recommend glitzy host costumes. Thrift stores are great places to find these.

- Say, "Welcome to Tic-Tac-Treeeeeeeeeeeat! The game where lunchboxes go from dull to delicious! This week we are starting a new Superkid Lesson series, so we thought it would be awesome to have a GAME series! So, for the next three weeks, we'll be playing 'Tic-Tac-Treat.' There's something really important you should know when playing this game. All the questions we'll be using in this game will come from our lesson the week before. So, pay very close attention today and the next few weeks!"

- Choose two Superkids. Read question No. 1. If the players know the answer, they should raise their hands. The first player to raise his or her hand may answer. If correct, allow the player to choose to be an X or O, and pick a lunchbox. Do not have Player 1 turn the lunchbox around; you'll do it for him or her. Use this time to hype things up, like a game-show host: "Will it be an X or an O? Let's find out!"

- After Player 1 has correctly answered a question and picked a box, ask a question of Player 2. If Player 2 is correct, he or she may choose a box. If not, play returns back to Player 1.

- Go back and forth this way until someone has three X's or three O's. At that time, declare, "We have a Tic-Tac-Treat!" Let the winning Superkid open the three winning lunchboxes and have the treats as the game prize.

- Because this game is rather involved, only one round is usually needed.

Game Goal:

Pay close attention to God's Word for opportunities to be blessed!

Final Word:

When we pay close attention to God's Word, there are lots of awesome "treats" waiting for us, even better than "Tic-Tac-Treats"!

Variation No. 1: Brown Paper Bags

Lunch-size brown paper bags could be used instead of lunchboxes for the game. Your children could even color or decorate them with stickers before the game to build their anticipation.

Variation No. 2: Family vs. Family

If you know of another family studying *Superkid Academy's The Heart of a Superkid Home Bible Study for Kids,* consider joining together—and facing off—for a fun evening of dinner and Tic-Tac-Treat. It's an exciting way to celebrate Bible study and godly friendships!

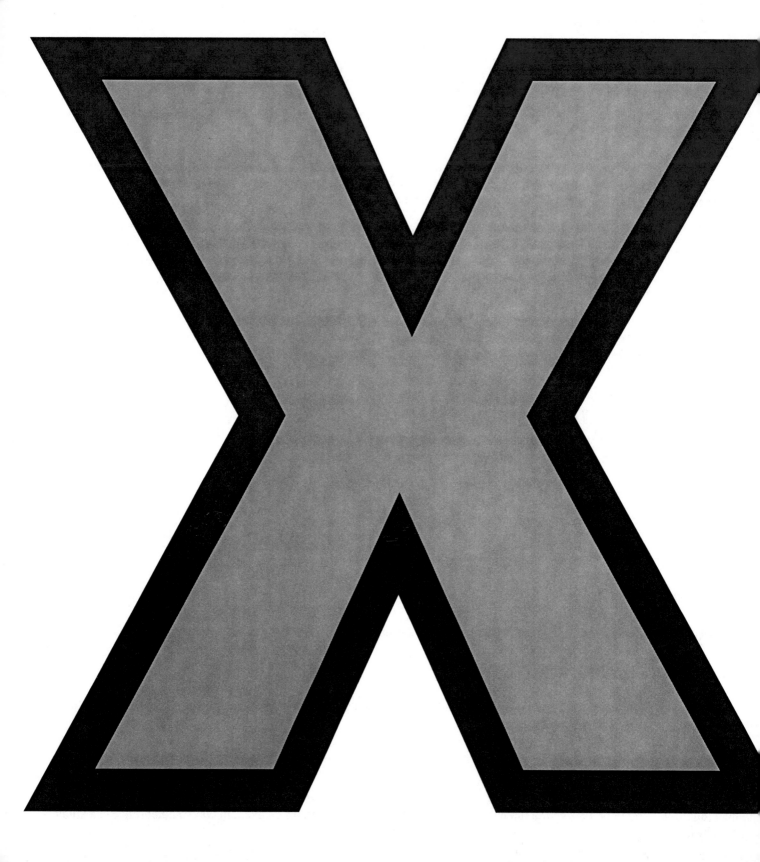

TIC-TAC-TREAT QUESTIONS: VOL. 4/WEEK 4

(Review Taken From Vol. 4/Week 3)

BIBLE LESSON:

#1 <u>Question:</u> <u>What did Adam and Eve do after they disobeyed God?</u>
Answer: They hid.

#2 <u>Question:</u> <u>Name one of the two things that happen when the devil gets his way.</u>
Answer: Secrets or hiding.

#3 <u>Question:</u> <u>What was the highest price God paid to get His children back?</u>
Answer: The Lamb slain before the beginning of the world, Jesus.

#4 <u>Question:</u> <u>Jesus brought us back to live in THE BLESSING of what place?</u>
Answer: The Garden of Eden.

#5 <u>Question:</u> <u>What kind of life does God want us to choose?</u>
Answer: The Sweet Life.

GIVING LESSON:

#6 <u>Question:</u> <u>In Luke 14, Jesus told us to invite what kind of people to our parties?</u>
Answer: The kind who never get invited: 'outsiders.'

#7 <u>Question:</u> <u>What happens when you reach out to outsiders?</u>
Answer: You'll be a blessing AND be blessed!

MEMORY VERSE:

#8 <u>Question:</u> <u>What was last week's memory verse?</u>
Answer: "The thief's purpose is to steal and kill and destroy. My purpose is to give them a rich and satisfying life." John 10:10

FOOD FUN:

#9 <u>Question:</u> <u>Just like Adam and Eve made a mess when they did things wrong, so did our cook. What did the cook do wrong?</u>
Answer: Exploded an egg in the microwave oven.

READ-ALOUD:

#10 <u>Question:</u> <u>What happened when John Mark told skater Nick about Jesus?</u>
Answer: Nick asked Jesus into his heart and joined a Christian skate club training for the X-Games.

TIC-TAC-TREAT (10 QUESTIONS TOTAL)

BIBLE LESSON: (5 questions)

#1 Q: _____

_____

A: _____

_____

#2 Q: _____

_____

A: _____

_____

#3 Q: _____

_____

A: _____

_____

#4 Q: _____

_____

A: _____

_____

#5 Q: _____

_____

A: _____

_____

Notes: _____

_____

_____

TIC-TAC-TREAT (10 QUESTIONS TOTAL)

GIVING LESSON: (2 questions)

#1 Q:_____

_____

A:_____

_____

#2 Q:_____

_____

A:_____

_____

MEMORY VERSE: (1 question)

#1 Q:_____

_____

A:_____

_____

WILD CARD: (2 questions)

#1 Q:_____

_____

A:_____

_____

#2 Q:_____

_____

A:_____

_____

ACTIVITY PAGE

HONOR WORD SEARCH

Memory Verse: But I will honor those who honor me, and I will despise those who think lightly of me.—1 Samuel 2:30b

Honor is an important part of living a successful life for God. In this word search, the word honor appears 15 times. See if you can find them!

ANSWER KEY

Notes: _____

_____

_____

_____

_____

_____

_____

_____

_____

_____

_____

_____

WEEK 5: OBEY YOUR PARENTS

 Memory Verse: Children, obey your parents because you belong to the Lord, for this is the right thing to do. "Honor your father and mother." This is the first commandment with a promise. —Ephesians 6:1-2

WEEK 5: SNAPSHOT — OBEY YOUR PARENTS

DAY	TYPE OF LESSON	LESSON TITLE	SUPPLIES
Day 1	Bible Lesson	Jesus at the Temple	None
Day 2	Object Lesson	Stay on Top	Large container with water, 10-12 Marbles, 1 Stick of modeling clay, Paper towels
Day 3	Giving Lesson	Who's Your Friend?	A pile of candy in bag, Resealable plastic snack bags, Paper and markers
Day 4	Read-Aloud	The Witness Zone: "All in the Family"	None
Day 5	Game Time	Tic-Tac-Treat	Refer to Week 4 supply list and replenish treats
Bonus	Activity Page	Temple Trip-Ups	1 Copy for each child

Lesson Introduction:

Let's help kids learn how to receive discipline! As you teach this lesson, help your children to understand the demand that God has placed on you, their parents, to teach, guide *and* discipline. Then, remind them that when two or more are in agreement (children and parents, where correction is concerned), the Lord's presence will be in the midst of them—now, that's effective discipline!

A great pictorial lesson is provided in talking about a swamp. With your words, "paint" a picture of mud, stink, snakes, flies, and don't forget the parasites: the invisible dangers. The grosser the description, (albeit interesting to the scientifically minded!), the greater impact you will see. The swamp is a great habitat for the animals created to live there but not a great environment for people! We were created for a different kind of life! When we disobey, it's like making our way through the muck of a swamp—it's hard, and there are many dangers lurking under the surface!

Make the choice to obey, and enjoy "The Sweet Life" God has promised!

Love,

Commander Kellie
Commander Kellie

Lesson Outline:

This week's lessons will focus on obedience and THE BLESSING that follows those who obey Jesus. Applying the Word of God will bring THE BLESSING into your family.

I. A SPECIAL PROMISE FROM GOD Exodus 20:12

a. Kids who obey and honor their parents get a reward.

b. It's the first commandment with a specific reward. That's important.

c. Living a long, full life is an "obedience" blessing from God.

II. PARENTS ARE GOD'S No. 1 GIFT TO KIDS

a. They help you receive wisdom and hear from God.

b. You should submit to their instruction and discipline. Proverbs 6:20

c. If you won't obey your parents, you won't obey God.

III. DON'T MISS OUT ON "THE SWEET LIFE" Ephesians 6:1-3

a. God's designed "The Sweet Life" for kids who honor and obey.

b. The way of the disobedient is like an impassable swamp. Proverbs 13:15 AMP

c. "The Sweet Life" or Swampy Life—it's your choice. God hates disobedience because it keeps you from "The Sweet Life." He wants good things for you!

Notes:_____

_____

_____

_____

_____

_____

_____

_____

_____

_____

_____

_____

DAY 1: BIBLE LESSON

JESUS AT THE TEMPLE

Memory Verse: *Children, obey your parents because you belong to the Lord, for this is the right thing to do. Honor your father and mother. This is the first commandment with a promise.* —Ephesians 6:1-2

Jesus is our best example of how to live. In this passage, your children will learn that Jesus obeyed His heavenly Father as He did His earthly parents. Exodus 20:12 teaches that those who honor their parents will be blessed. In fact, it is the first commandment that promises a specific reward—long, full life. That's a promise for *your* children, too!

Read Luke 2:41-52:
Jesus Speaks With the Teachers

Every year Jesus' parents went to Jerusalem for the Passover festival. When Jesus was twelve years old, they attended the festival, as usual. After the celebration was over, they started home to Nazareth, but Jesus stayed behind in Jerusalem. His parents didn't miss him at first, because they assumed he was among the other travelers. But when he didn't show up that evening, they started looking for him among their relatives and friends.

When they couldn't find him, they went back to Jerusalem to search for him there. Three days later, they finally discovered him in the Temple, sitting among the religious teachers, listening to them and asking questions. All who heard him were amazed at his understanding and his answers.

His parents didn't know what to think. "Son," his mother said to him, "why have you done this to us? Your father and I have been frantic, searching for you everywhere."

"But why did you need to search?" he asked. "Didn't you know that I must be in my Father's house?" But they didn't understand what he meant.

Then he returned to Nazareth with them and was obedient to them. And his mother stored all these things in her heart.

Jesus grew in wisdom and in stature and in favor with God and all the people.

Discussion Questions:

1. **Describe three things that happened in this story.**
   Answers will vary, but use this time of discussion to make sure your children understand the passage.

2. **Why was Jesus at the Temple?**
   He was listening and talking to the teachers.

3. **What did He say to His mother, Mary, when she asked why He had remained in Jerusalem?**
   He said He was in His Father's house.

4. **Which Father was He talking about?**
   He was talking about His heavenly Father.

5. **When He left with Mary and Joseph, what was His attitude? Was He angry and resentful, or was He respectful and obedient?**
   He was respectful and obedient.

6. **What can we learn about how children should respond to their parents?**
Children should be respectful and obedient to their parents.

7. **What are some areas where it is difficult to obey parents?**
Accept all answers. Writing them on a piece of paper might be easier for some than answering verbally.

Notes: _____

_____

_____

_____

_____

_____

_____

_____

_____

_____

_____

_____

_____

_____

_____

_____

_____

_____

_____

_____

_____

_____

_____

_____

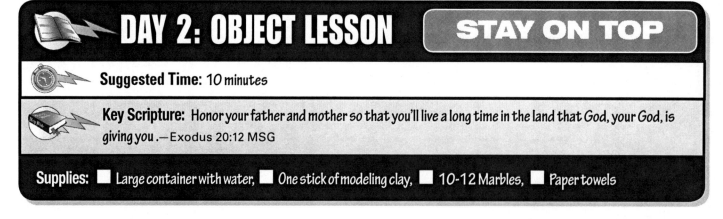

DAY 2: OBJECT LESSON — STAY ON TOP

Suggested Time: *10 minutes*

Key Scripture: *Honor your father and mother so that you'll live a long time in the land that God, your God, is giving you.*—Exodus 20:12 MSG

Supplies: ☐ Large container with water, ☐ One stick of modeling clay, ☐ 10-12 Marbles, ☐ Paper towels

Lesson Instructions:

I have some supplies here that most of you have played with before: marbles and modeling clay.

If I took this clay and made it into a ball *(begin forming the clay as you talk)* and then put it into this water, would it float or sink? *(Get response from the kids and then place the clay in the water to sink to the bottom.)*

What about these marbles, will they float or sink? *(Repeat the same scenario as with the clay.)*

This lump of clay reminds me of children who are disobedient to their parents. When you choose not to obey, did you know that you are choosing a hard life that is filled with problems? Your life could end up like this clay—just lying on the bottom, going nowhere.

But, let's say you decide to make a change—you decide to follow what God's Word says and respect your dad (or mom) and me by being obedient. *(Retrieve the clay and marbles from the water and dry them off.)* Now, we can take this same clay and reshape it and see what kind of difference it will make. *(Shape clay into boat or a bowl shape and place on the surface of the water.)* Now, instead of sinking to the bottom, the clay is floating on top of the water. It's the same clay, it weighs the same as before, but because the shape is different, it is floating instead of sinking.

Kids, this clay is like our hearts. When we decide to honor our parents, we will have lives that are filled with God's goodness—lives that stay on top instead of sinking to the bottom.

And, do you know that there are bonuses to living this way?

Let's say these marbles are the rewards God promises to kids who obey their moms and dads. In Exodus 20:12, it says that when we honor our father and mother, God promises we will live a long time *(place two or three marbles in your clay boat)* and we will own land *(add more marbles to the boat, making sure not to sink it).*

How cool is that? It's easy to see that, in God's opinion, it doesn't take much to stay on top of things. Just obey your parents, and the Lord will be sure to load up your boat with His goodness!

Variation: Becoming a Vessel

Allow kids to make other shapes than your original boat. Typically, someone will design something that is destined to sink. Take this opportunity to remind them that God has special plans and designs for their lives, but they have to allow Him to shape and mold them (through obedience) into the "vessel" He's designed them to be!

DAY 3: GIVING LESSON — WHO'S YOUR FRIEND?

Suggested Time: 15 minutes

Offering Scripture: Tell them to go after God, who piles on all the riches we could ever manage.—1 Timothy 6:17 MSG

Supplies: ☐ A pile of candy in a bag   ☐ Resealable plastic snack bags   ☐ Paper and markers

Lesson Instructions:

Today, I want each of you to give me a hand with a little giving experiment. In this bag there is some delicious candy. Wouldn't you love some?

Well, this is your assignment: I would like you to give as much of this candy away to your friends as you like. Take your time as you decide who you'd like to give it to. You can make small cards to go with the candy. *(While kids are preparing these cards and resealable plastic snack bags, it's quite likely they're going to want to eat some of the candy. That's totally acceptable! Or you might even find an older sibling nudging a younger one to write them a note. Let it happen: It teaches the lesson!)*

I would like to read you a verse from 1 Timothy that will help us think the right way about our God. In 1 Timothy 6:17, it says, "Tell them to go after God, who piles on all the riches we could ever manage." Did you hear that? Of course we know our heavenly Father is always looking for ways to bless us, but this verse shows us that's not what we should be focusing on. Who does it say we should be going after? It says to go after God! Did you realize that when we love the Lord and He's the One our attention is on, our lives will be piled high with everything we need? So, as you prepare to give your candy treats away today, remember the reason we are giving is because we love our heavenly Father, the One who is so generous to His kids, and we want to bless others like He blesses us!

Discussion Questions:

Allow the following questions to start discussions between you and your children. There are no right or wrong answers, so use this time to mold your children's character, enhance your communication and build your relationships.

1. **Were you tempted to take a few pieces of candy?**

2. **What did you think about giving ALL the candy away?**

3. **How does giving something away make you feel, especially when it's something you like?**

Notes: _____

_____

_____

_____

DAY 4: READ-ALOUD

THE WITNESS ZONE: "ALL IN THE FAMILY"

Suggested Time: 15 minutes

Memory Verse: Children, obey your parents because you belong to the Lord, for this is the right thing to do. "Honor your father and mother." This is the first commandment with a promise. —Ephesians 6:1-2

Lesson Instructions:

You are about to enter a zone unlike any other, where normal life becomes anything but normal and everyday conversations go from ordinary to shocking in the blink of an eye. It's a place where eternal choices are made—where faith meets fear, and boldness meets hesitation. It's a zone where Superkids can become history makers or bolt like a runaway train. Buckle your seat belts and hold on for the ride. You are about to enter... "The Witness Zone."

There's your mother. She's sitting at a table, going through bills, talking to herself. Money must be tight.

"Why do all these bills have to come all at once?" Mom asks. Then, "Maybe it won't be as bad as I think. Let's see...." She shuffles through the envelopes. "Water bill, electricity, car, credit card, phone bill...oh my!"

Then, Mom does the unthinkable. She pulls out the calculator and adds up the bills. "$765!" she shouts. "Well, I'll just have to take it out of savings."

But then, Mom checks her savings account balance. "$29?! That can't be right...oh...yes, that's right." She sighs. "How will we ever make it?"

Finally, you decide to come around the corner, and your mother sees you. Her eyes hold steady.

"Mom?"

"Go clean your room," she says.

You ask, "What did the bank...?"

"Didn't you hear me?" Mom interrupts. "I said, go clean your room. *Now!*"

You know she's had a hard time, but it doesn't seem fair that she's getting mad at you. It's not your fault. You shout, *"Fine! I'm going!"* and run up the stairs.

(Discuss what your children think about how the child in the lesson responded. What do they think about the situation? How would they have handled it? Can they identify with it?)

Well, that was one way to handle it. There's mom, under great pressure to pay the bills, short on money. And instead of honoring her, you angrily talked back, making "The Witness Zone" door slam shut. But all is not lost. Let's see what happens when you show your mom love and respect instead. Let's read the story again, but this time, change the ending.

Alternate Ending:

There's your mother. She's sitting at a table, going through bills, talking to herself. Money must be tight.

"Why do all these bills have to come all at once?" Mom asks. Then, "Maybe it won't be as bad as I think. Let's see...." She shuffles through the envelopes. "Water bill, electricity, car, credit card, phone bill…oh my!"

Then Mom does the unthinkable. She pulls out the calculator and adds up the bills. "$765!" she shouts. "Well, I'll just have to take it out of savings."

But then Mom checks her savings account balance. "$29?! That can't be right…oh…yes, that's right." She sighs. "How will we ever make it?"

Finally, you decide to come around the corner, and your mother sees you. Her eyes hold steady.

"Mom?"

"Go clean your room," she says.

You say, "Yes, ma'am. But may I ask you a question first?"

Your mother doesn't drop her eyes. "Make it fast."

You ask, "May I pray for you?"

And just like that, it happens. Mom smiles. She stretches out a hand toward you. You hold hands and bow your heads.

You pray, "Lord, I thank You that You meet all of our needs according to Your riches in glory. And right now, You are working to bring in the money Mom needs to pay these bills. Thank You for Your peace on our family, in Jesus' Name. Amen." Then with a smile, you add, "We're going to be OK, Mom. God's taking care of us."

Mom kisses you on the forehead. "Thank you, kiddo. I don't know what I would do without you."

There you have it! One story, two different endings. Another opened door, another victory. A challenge given, and a challenge met. When you choose God's way and honor your mom, blessings are already on the way. It's a zone that challenges every Superkid to ask this question, "What will I do next time I enter…'The Witness Zone'?!"

Discussion Questions:

Use these questions as conversation starters. Enjoy this time of talking, listening and discipling your children.

1. **What did you think about this story? Could you relate?**
2. **Can you think of a time when I have been short-tempered with you and you didn't understand why?**
3. **How have you responded to me?**
4. **Let your children know that sometimes adults have difficult things to deal with. Explain that parents are human too, and they need prayer just like everyone else.**

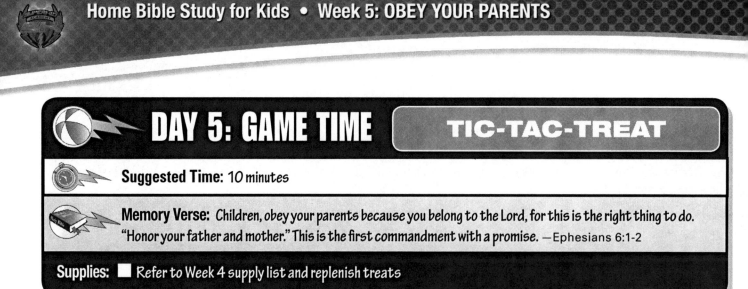

DAY 5: GAME TIME — TIC-TAC-TREAT

Suggested Time: 10 minutes

Memory Verse: Children, obey your parents because you belong to the Lord, for this is the right thing to do. "Honor your father and mother." This is the first commandment with a promise. —Ephesians 6:1-2

Supplies: ☐ Refer to Week 4 supply list and replenish treats

Game Instructions:

Refer to Week 4 game instructions and variations.

Game Goal:

Pay close attention to God's Word for opportunities to be blessed!

Final Word:

When we pay close attention to God's Word there are lots of awesome "treats" waiting for us, even better than "Tic-Tac-Treats"!

Refer to Week 4 for Tic-Tac-Treat letters to copy (X's and O's).

Notes: _____

_____

_____

_____

_____

_____

_____

_____

_____

_____

_____

_____

TIC-TAC-TREAT QUESTIONS: VOL. 4/WEEK 5

(Review Taken From Vol. 4/Week 4)

BIBLE LESSON:

#1 <u>Question:</u> <u>What does "honor" mean?</u>
Answer: Respect, regard or esteem.

#2 <u>Question:</u> <u>What are the three steps to show honor?</u>
Answer: Listen, submit to and obey.

#3 <u>Question:</u> <u>How did Saul dishonor God?</u>
Answer: He didn't submit to or obey God.

#4 <u>Question:</u> <u>Who always honors God?</u>
Answer: Jesus!

#5 <u>Question:</u> <u>How did Jesus honor His Father?</u>
Answer: He listened, submitted and obeyed.

GIVING LESSON:

#6 <u>Question:</u> <u>Instead of worrying about your needs, what should you do?</u>
Answer: Pray about everything (let God know your concerns—Philippians 4:6).

#7 <u>Question:</u> <u>What "growing exercise" did we do?</u>
Answer: Wrote down things we were trusting God to take care of and put it in an envelope.

MEMORY VERSE:

#8 <u>Question:</u> <u>What was last week's memory verse?</u>
Answer: "But I will honor those who honor me, and I will despise those who think lightly of me."
1 Samuel 2:30b

FOOD FUN:

#9 <u>Question:</u> <u>Just like the secret ingredient in our chocolate milk treat last week, what is the secret</u>
<u>ingredient to honoring God?</u>
Answer: The secret ingredient is obeying His Word.

OBJECT LESSON:

#10 <u>Question:</u> <u>In the Object Lesson last week, you learned three easy ways to honor God. Name one of them.</u>
Answer: 1. Pleasing Him (even consider the way you dress).
2. Respect His Word (take care of your Bible and obey it!).
3. Care about what God thinks, even if friends disagree.

TIC-TAC-TREAT (10 QUESTIONS TOTAL)

BIBLE LESSON: (5 questions)

#1 Q: _____

_____

A: _____

_____

#2 Q: _____

_____

A: _____

_____

#3 Q: _____

_____

A: _____

_____

#4 Q: _____

_____

A: _____

_____

#5 Q: _____

_____

A: _____

_____

Notes: _____

_____

_____

TIC-TAC-TREAT (10 QUESTIONS TOTAL)

GIVING LESSON: (2 questions)

#1 Q:_____

_____

A:_____

_____

#2 Q:_____

_____

A:_____

_____

MEMORY VERSE: (1 question)

#1 Q:_____

_____

A:_____

_____

FOOD FUN: (1 question)

#1 Q:_____

_____

A:_____

_____

WILD CARD: (1 question)

#1 Q:_____

_____

A:_____

_____

ACTIVITY PAGE

TEMPLE TRIP-UPS

Memory Verse: *Children, obey your parents because you belong to the Lord, for this is the right thing to do.* "Honor your father and mother." This is the first commandment with a promise. —Ephesians 6:1-2

In Luke 2:41-52 you learned that as a boy, Jesus visited the Temple and talked to the leaders. In the pictures below of Jesus in the Temple, everything is identical. Or is it? Find 10 differences between the two pictures.

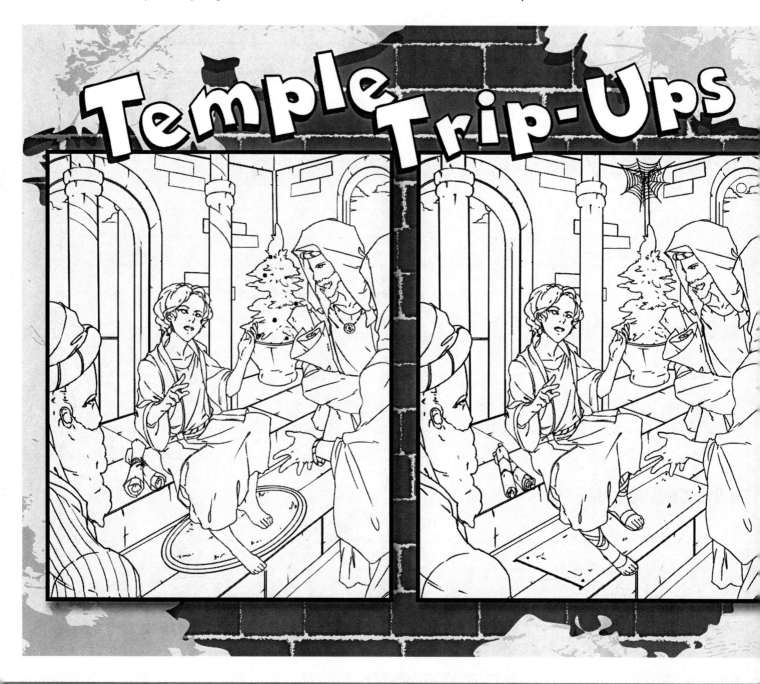

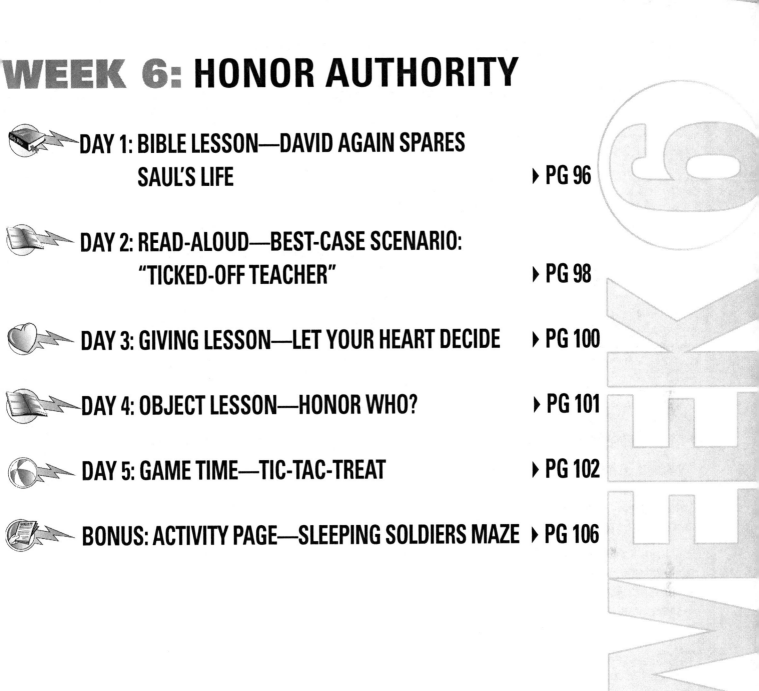

WEEK 6: HONOR AUTHORITY

 Memory Verse: Everyone must submit to governing authorities. For all authority comes from God, and those in positions of authority have been placed there by God. —Romans 13:1

WEEK 6: SNAPSHOT — HONOR AUTHORITY

DAY	TYPE OF LESSON	LESSON TITLE	SUPPLIES
Day 1	Bible Lesson	David Again Spares Saul's Life	None
Day 2	Read-Aloud	Best-Case Scenario: "Ticked-Off Teacher"	None
Day 3	Giving Lesson	Let Your Heart Decide	2 Containers: one labeled "mind" and one labeled "heart," $5 Bill, A nickel, Big candy bar, 1 Piece of gum, 1 Nice (new) toy, 1 Cheap (new) toy (dollar store variety)
Day 4	Object Lesson	Honor Who?	Teacher costume ("smart" glasses, bow tie, clipboard, ruler), Pastor costume (dress shirt, tie, Bible), Police or fireman costume (police hat, badge, uniform shirt, handcuffs, fireman's hat, boots), President costume (dark suit, coat, American flag), Table, 4 Sheets or towels
Day 5	Game Time	Tic-Tac-Treat	Refer to Week 4 supply list and replenish treats
Bonus	Activity Page	Sleeping Soldiers Maze	1 Copy for each child

Lesson Introduction:

Teaching our kids to honor authority is so very important today. Our greatest reason for honoring authority is that God asked us to! The resulting peaceful, godly life is a blessed one!

It is a great thing to encourage our kids to not only show honor by listening and obeying, but by addressing our authorities and referring to them respectfully. Guide kids to think out of the box: Who are your authorities? (Parents, teachers, policemen, firemen, pastors, babysitters, elders and, of course, government leaders.) Then, discuss how we should refer to those in authority. Should they be addressed by their first names? Should we use derogatory terms such as "cop" or "old lady"? Never!

Teaching children a proper greeting for those in authority, spoken respectfully and with eye contact, is a valuable life skill that we should teach from a biblical perspective. Adding a proper term of respect such as Mr., Mrs., President, etc., is a social grace as well as a principle derived from biblical teaching.

One more very important point: It doesn't matter whether we like the people in authority or agree with the things they do. We are to show respect and honor for their positions of authority and offices they hold because when we do things God's way, we are honoring Him. People will see a difference in our kids and begin to honor God in us. And most importantly, God will honor us when we honor His way of doing things.

Love,

Commander Kellie

Commander Kellie

Lesson Outline:

This week, you will be approaching the challenging topic of authority and God's plan for all of us to honor those in authority. It's a great opportunity to make God the center of your family's discussions about politics and current events. Enjoy seeing where these discussions will lead your family!

I. HONOR AND RESPECT ALL AUTHORITY 1 Peter 2:12-17

    a. When we live honorably it causes others to honor God.

    b. He asked you to do it for His sake (on His behalf).

    c. You honor God's request when you respect authority.

II. GOD'S WORD TELLS US TO PRAY FOR OUR LEADERS 1 Timothy 2:1-4

    a. Pray for and give thanks for your leaders—whether you like them or not. The result is peaceable, godly lives.

    b. This is good (it's an act of giving) and it pleases God—that's reason enough for us to do it!

    c. He has a great purpose for us to pray—He wants everyone to be saved.

III. ALL AUTHORITY IS A GIFT FROM GOD Romans 13:1-7

    a. When you rebel against them, it is the same as rebelling against God.

    b. Don't be afraid of authorities—as God's servants they are there to protect you.

    c. Decide today to give respect and honor to those in authority—listen, submit and obey.

Notes:_____

_____

_____

_____

_____

_____

_____

_____

_____

_____

_____

DAY 1: BIBLE LESSON — DAVID AGAIN SPARES SAUL'S LIFE

Memory Verse: *Everyone must submit to governing authorities. For all authority comes from God, and those in positions of authority have been placed there by God.*—Romans 13:1

As you read this account with your children, it's important to remind them that Saul was the king whom God had chosen—and rejected—because of his disobedience. At the time of this story, David already knew that he was chosen by God to be the next king of Israel. Even so, David chose to wait on God's timing and let God bring His promises into fulfillment. What an amazing testimony of utter trust in God and His powerful Word!

Read I Samuel 26:3-12:
Honoring God's Anointed

Saul camped along the road beside the hill of Hakilah, near Jeshimon, where David was hiding. When David learned that Saul had come after him into the wilderness, he sent out spies to verify the report of Saul's arrival.

David slipped over to Saul's camp one night to look around. Saul and Abner son of Ner, the commander of his army, were sleeping inside a ring formed by the slumbering warriors. "Who will volunteer to go in there with me?" David asked Ahimelech the Hittite and Abishai son of Zeruiah, Joab's brother.

"I'll go with you," Abishai replied.

So David and Abishai went right into Saul's camp and found him asleep, with his spear stuck in the ground beside his head. Abner and the soldiers were lying asleep around him. "God has surely handed your enemy over to you this time!" Abishai whispered to David. "Let me pin him to the ground with one thrust of the spear; I won't need to strike twice!"

"No!" David said. "Don't kill him. For who can remain innocent after attacking the Lord's anointed one? Surely the Lord will strike Saul down someday, or he will die of old age or in battle. The Lord forbid that I should kill the one he has anointed! But take his spear and that jug of water beside his head, and then let's get out of here!"

So David took the spear and jug of water that were near Saul's head. Then he and Abishai got away without anyone seeing them or even waking up, because the Lord had put Saul's men into a deep sleep.

Discussion Questions:

1. **Who was the king of Israel at the time of this story?**
   Saul

2. **Who is on the run from the king?**
   David

3. **Whom had God chosen to be the next king of Israel?**
   David

4. **Retell the story in your own words.**
   Acceptable paraphrases are great.

5. **Why did David refuse to kill Saul, even when presented with the perfect opportunity?**
Saul was God's anointed, the chosen king of Israel and David honored, or respected, that.

6. **What lesson do you think God wants us to learn from David's example?**
We are to respect those in authority, even when they are unkind, unfair or try to persecute us.

Notes: _____

_____

_____

_____

_____

_____

_____

_____

_____

_____

_____

_____

_____

_____

_____

_____

_____

_____

_____

_____

_____

_____

_____

_____

_____

DAY 2: READ-ALOUD

BEST-CASE SCENARIO: "TICKED-OFF TEACHER"

Suggested Time: 15 minutes

Memory Verse: Everyone must submit to governing authorities. For all authority comes from God, and those in positions of authority have been placed there by God.—Romans 13:1

Lesson Instructions:

There are two people you're about to meet. Their lives are about to clash…and how they interact with each other will either result in lots of trouble…or lots of good. Let's see what they do.

First, there's 11-year-old Lexie. Her hobbies include kickboxing, golf and popping her knuckles. Her favorite phrase is, "Just do it."

Lexie is about to walk into the classroom of her Sunday school teacher, Mrs. Redding. Mrs. Redding won't tell anyone her age, and her favorite phrase is, "In your seats!" Her hobbies include reading, watching *Animal Planet®,* and baking giant chocolate-chip cookies.

Today, Mrs. Redding is mad; in fact, she was running late to church and has had little or no time to prepare for today's lessons. Can Lexie refuse to get a bad attitude and help her ticked-off teacher? Let's find out.

Lexie is the first to her classroom and Mrs. Redding is there alone, flipping through papers.

"Oh my, oh my, oh my," says Mrs. Redding. "Not enough time at all."

"Mrs. Redding?" Lexie calls. Her Sunday school teacher looks up. Lexie continues, "Uh…um…"

"Uh, um, what?" Mrs. Redding asks.

"Are you OK?" asks Lexie.

"Sure…great. Why wouldn't I be?" Mrs. Redding taps the stack of papers on her desk. Then tears a page off the top, crumples it up and tosses it at the wall.

Lexie continues, "It's just that you seem a little upset. Is there anything I can pray with you about?"

Mrs. Redding tilts her head. "For one, you could pray my husband gets a brain."

Lexie's eyes grow big. "He needs a brain transplant?"

That gets a laugh out of Mrs. Redding. "No, we just had a disagreement this morning."

Lexie steps forward. "I guess I could pray with you about that. Do you mind?"

"I…" Mrs. Redding is clearly caught off guard. "No, not at all."

Lexie smiles and grabs Mrs. Redding's hand. They bow heads. "Lord, I ask that You would give Mrs. Redding and her husband peace. You said that You want us to lead peaceable lives without fighting. Help soften their hearts to be patient and forgive each other, like You forgive us. In Jesus' Name. Amen."

Mrs. Redding looks up and gives Lexie a big hug. "Thank you so much, Lexie. I already feel better."

"You're welcome," Lexie says. "Is there anything I can help you with? It looks like it'll be a few minutes before anyone else arrives."

"That would be great!" says Mrs. Redding. "Could you put these papers in front of every seat while I write some key words on the whiteboard?"

Lexie grabs the papers. "No problem."

She did it! A "Best-Case Scenario." Instead of being mad at Mrs. "In Your Seats!" Redding, Lexie kickboxed anger—which was easy, once she remembered that even leaders may be grouchy and need our prayers.

Not only did Mrs. Redding get happier, but also Lexie's prayers worked! Mrs. Redding's husband brought in a bouquet of flowers before Sunday school started, which made her so happy that she didn't order everyone into their seats. And if that wasn't good enough, Mrs. Redding asked Lexie if she wanted to be her special assistant each week in Sunday school because she did such a great job. Talk about a "Best-Case Scenario!" Only with God could it get as good as that!

Discussion Questions:

Use these questions as conversation starters. Let this be a time of talking and listening to your children.

1. **How did Lexie show Mrs. Redding respect and honor?**

2. **Why is it important to show respect to those in authority, like teachers and pastors and government officials?**

3. **Have you ever experienced being with an adult who was in a bad mood? What happened?**

4. **How did you respond?**

5. **After reading this story today, would you change your response?**

Notes:_____

_____

_____

_____

_____

_____

_____

_____

_____

_____

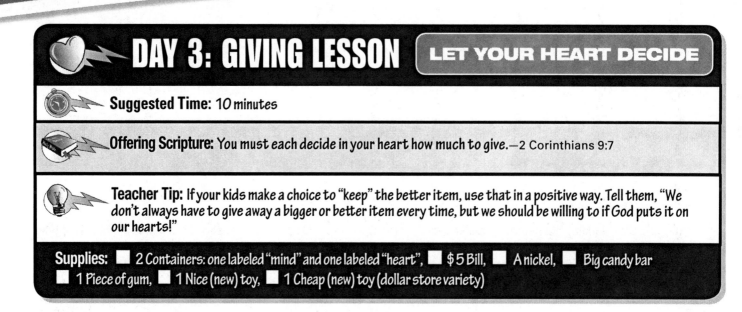

DAY 3: GIVING LESSON — LET YOUR HEART DECIDE

Suggested Time: 10 minutes

Offering Scripture: You must each decide in your heart how much to give.—2 Corinthians 9:7

Teacher Tip: If your kids make a choice to "keep" the better item, use that in a positive way. Tell them, "We don't always have to give away a bigger or better item every time, but we should be willing to if God puts it on our hearts!"

Supplies: ☐ 2 Containers: one labeled "mind" and one labeled "heart", ☐ $5 Bill, ☐ A nickel, ☐ Big candy bar ☐ 1 Piece of gum, ☐ 1 Nice (new) toy, ☐ 1 Cheap (new) toy (dollar store variety)

Lesson Instructions:

Are you ready for a little pop quiz? OK, don't get concerned, these questions are pretty easy—multiple choice. I am going to need two of you to help me out with this quiz. Who's good at taking tests?

Here are two containers, one called "mind" and one called "heart." Before we get started with the quiz, I need to read a verse from 2 Corinthians 9:7, "You must each decide in your heart how much to give."

This little test is going to be called "Mind vs. Heart." I will give each of you an item, and you are to decide which one your heart would tell you to give away and which one your mind might say was the one to give away. You will then put your item in the right container. *(Start by handing the big candy bar to one child and the piece of gum to the other.)*

Which do you think your heart would say is the right one to give away? *(Let the players decide and place their item where they think it should go.)*

Your heart would probably say the candy bar would be the thing to give away since it's the more generous thing to do, right? But sometimes our head tells us we should keep the best for ourselves and only give away smaller things. *(Lead the kids through the rest of the items, pairing the money together and the toys together.)*

Kids, I love the way God's Word tells us we must decide in our hearts what to give. God tells us that, because He knows when we follow our hearts, we will never go wrong. And, with Jesus in our hearts, our hearts are bound to be generous! Let's be generous with God as we bring our offerings to Him.

Notes: _____

_____

_____

_____

_____

_____

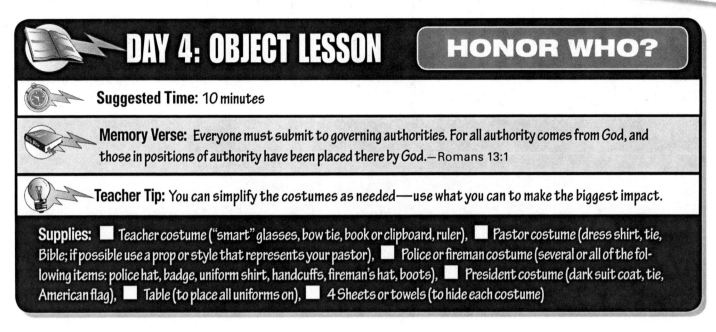

DAY 4: OBJECT LESSON · HONOR WHO?

Suggested Time: 10 minutes

Memory Verse: Everyone must submit to governing authorities. For all authority comes from God, and those in positions of authority have been placed there by God. —Romans 13:1

Teacher Tip: You can simplify the costumes as needed—use what you can to make the biggest impact.

Supplies: ☐ Teacher costume ("smart" glasses, bow tie, book or clipboard, ruler), ☐ Pastor costume (dress shirt, tie, Bible; if possible use a prop or style that represents your pastor), ☐ Police or fireman costume (several or all of the following items: police hat, badge, uniform shirt, handcuffs, fireman's hat, boots), ☐ President costume (dark suit coat, tie, American flag), ☐ Table (to place all uniforms on), ☐ 4 Sheets or towels (to hide each costume)

Lesson Instructions:

Ask for volunteers to help with today's lesson. Choose one person or arrange for a guest to come and be your person of interest. As the guest makes an entrance, ask the other kids the following questions:

- What is this person's occupation? How can you tell?

- Who do they work for?

- Who pays their salary?

- What is the proper way to address them?

- Have you ever seen anyone address them in a rude, improper manner?

As you go through the various costumes you've prepared (teacher, policeman, fireman, pastor, president), remind kids that God wants us to honor all those in authority, even if they're not nice or if we don't agree with some of the things they do.

Wrap up by reviewing the lesson and the memory verse, Romans 13:1, that God has ordained all authority, and we must respect people in those positions with a gracious attitude and hearts that reflect God's presence in our lives!

Variation: Name Tags

Make it even more personal to your family by adding name tags to your "characters." Officer Smith or Pastor Joe might have a bigger impact (and get a few chuckles from your kids) if they see that you're impersonating real people whom they know.

Notes: _____

_____

_____

DAY 5: GAME TIME — TIC-TAC-TREAT

Suggested Time: 10 minutes

Memory Verse: Everyone must submit to governing authorities. For all authority comes from God, and those in positions of authority have been placed there by God.—Romans 13:1

Supplies: ☐ Refer to Week 4 supply list and replenish treats

Game Instructions:

Refer to Week 4 game instructions and variations.

Game Goal:

Pay close attention to God's Word for opportunities to be blessed!

Final Word:

When we pay close attention to God's Word there are lots of awesome "treats" waiting for us, even better than "Tic-Tac-Treats"!

Refer to Week 4 for Tic-Tac-Treat letters to copy (X's and O's).

Notes: _____

_____

_____

_____

_____

_____

_____

_____

_____

_____

_____

_____

TIC-TAC-TREAT QUESTIONS: VOL. 4/WEEK 6

(Review Taken From Vol. 4/Week 5)

BIBLE LESSON:

#1 Question: List one obedience blessing you get from God when you obey your parents.

Answer: I live a long life.

#2 Question: Who is God's No. 1 gift to me?

Answer: My parents.

#3 Question: When you disobey your parents, things get hard. What kind of life do we call this?

Answer: "Swampy Life."

#4 Question: Who else are you disobeying when you don't obey your parents?

Answer: God.

#5 Question: What kind of life do you get when you choose to obey your parents?

Answer: "The Sweet Life."

GIVING LESSON:

#6 Question: Philippians 4:6 says, "Don't worry about anything; instead _____ about everything."

Answer: Pray.

#7 Question: Who should we go after the most?

Answer: GOD!

MEMORY VERSE:

#8 Question: What was last week's memory verse?

Answer: "Children, obey your parents because you belong to the Lord, for this is the right thing to do. 'Honor your father and mother.' This is the first commandment with a promise." Ephesians 6:1-2

OBJECT LESSON:

#9 Question: What was the experiment last week? What did it mean?

Answer: Clay in a ball shape sinks, but when shaped correctly, it floats. This is like kids who obey; obedience shapes us for success!

READ-ALOUD:

#10 Question: How did the mother in the story react when the daughter was respectful and offered to pray for her mother instead of getting angry and stomping upstairs to clean her room?

Answer: The mother's attitude changed and she became more cheerful.

TIC-TAC-TREAT (10 QUESTIONS TOTAL)

BIBLE LESSON: (5 questions)

#1 Q: _____

_____

A: _____

_____

#2 Q: _____

_____

A: _____

_____

#3 Q: _____

_____

A: _____

_____

#4 Q: _____

_____

A: _____

_____

#5 Q: _____

_____

A: _____

_____

Notes: _____

_____

_____

TIC-TAC-TREAT (10 QUESTIONS TOTAL)

GIVING LESSON: (2 questions)

#1 Q:_____

_____

A:_____

_____

#2 Q:_____

_____

A:_____

_____

MEMORY VERSE: (1 question)

#1 Q:_____

_____

A:_____

_____

WILD CARD: (2 questions)

#1 Q:_____

_____

A:_____

_____

#2 Q:_____

_____

A:_____

_____

 **ACTIVITY PAGE** | **SLEEPING SOLDIERS MAZE**

Memory Verse: Everyone must submit to governing authorities. For all authority comes from God, and those in positions of authority have been placed there by God.—Romans 13:1

In your Bible Lesson this week, you learned that David sneaked up on King Saul while he was sleeping. Help him do it again in this maze, but be sure to avoid the sleeping soldiers!

WEEK 7: HONOR AND OBEY THE HOLY SPIRIT

 Memory Verse: Trust in the Lord with all your heart, do not depend on your own understanding. Seek His will in all you do, and He will show you which path to take.— Proverbs 3:5-6

WEEK 7: SNAPSHOT

HONOR AND OBEY THE HOLY SPIRIT

DAY	TYPE OF LESSON	LESSON TITLE	SUPPLIES
Day 1	Bible Lesson	Ananias and Sapphira	None
Day 2	Read-Aloud	The Witness Zone: "Friends in Tough Places"	None
Day 3	Giving Lesson	Pitching In	Ready-made pudding cup, 1 Box "kid-friendly" cereal, 1 Juice box, 1 Clear glass, 1 Drinking straw, More items for additional children
Day 4	Food Fun	Dip Into the Holy Spirit	Microwave oven, Medium-sized glass bowl, Large mixing spoon, Microwave-safe plastic wrap, Potholders, 1 Minced garlic clove, 1/2 Cup mayonnaise, 1 Cup sour cream, 3/4 Cup canned artichoke hearts, 1/4 Cup chopped green chilies, 1 10-Ounce package of frozen chopped spinach, 3/4 Cup parmesan cheese, 1/8 Teaspoon paprika, Cooking spray, 1 Package of pita bread or crackers, YouTube® clip of a Popeye® cartoon
Day 5	Game Time	Tic-Tac-Treat	Refer to Week 4 supply list and replenish treats
Bonus	Activity Page	Jerusalem Marketplace Look-and-Find	1 Copy for each child

Lesson Introduction:

Honoring Jesus' intention in sending the Holy Spirit includes receiving Him and the gift of speaking in tongues. The Holy Spirit (according to Jesus) is crucial to our walk with the Lord. How can you follow someone you can't see or hear? The Holy Spirit is Jesus' revealing agent (John 14-16). He tells us things that Jesus wants us to know (John 16:12-13). He searches the plan (the secret things) of God for us and tells us what to do (1 Corinthians 2:9-10).

Give your children the opportunity to receive the infilling of the Holy Spirit today. Then help the kids honor the gift! I've taught kids to never be timid when speaking in tongues. They are giving their voices to speak God's Words—His will for their lives. Encourage this often. Sometimes, at random times during your devotionals and worship times, say, "Let's pray in the spirit," and then encourage their boldness. As the kids learn to give Him their voices, they will become more proficient at hearing His voice. Obeying becomes an obvious thing to do!

Love,

Commander Kellie

Commander Kellie

Lesson Outline:

This week will provide a focus to honoring the Holy Spirit. You'll enjoy focusing on the often ignored third person of the Trinity, the Holy Spirit. Look for ways for the Holy Spirit to lead you and your children as you study and tune in to Him!

I. THE HOLY SPIRIT IS HONORED WHEN YOU RELY ON HIM

a. Honor Him as a precious gift from Jesus to help you. John 14:15-18, 26-27

b. The Holy Spirit is the best Guide to show those who trust and rely on Him which path to take every day. Proverbs 3:5-6

c. He will guide you into truth, tell you about the future and give you messages from Jesus! John 16:12-15

II. THE HOLY SPRIT IS HONORED WHEN YOU LET HIM HELP YOU

a. He helps us in every area of weakness. Romans 8:26

b. Let Him help you live honorably. Ephesians 4:23-24

c. Honoring Him does not bring Him sorrow. Ephesians 4:25-32

d. Obey what He tells you to do. Galatians 5:16

III. HONOR THE HOLY SPIRIT BY WELCOMING HIM IN

a. The Holy Spirit is honored when you hear His call and give Him your time. Psalm 27:8-9

b. Jesus gives "living water" to anyone who asks. John 7:38-39

c. We honor the Holy Spirit by inviting Him to fill us up.

d. He is honored when you give Him your voice; never be timid! You are praying His Words!

Notes:_____

_____

_____

_____

_____

_____

_____

_____

DAY 1: BIBLE LESSON

ANANIAS AND SAPPHIRA

Memory Verse: Trust in the Lord with all your heart, do not depend on your own understanding. Seek His will in all you do, and He will show you which path to take. —Proverbs 3:5-6

As you read today's lesson with your children, difficult questions may arise. The punishment for dishonoring the Holy Spirit seems brutal, but it's a great discussion launcher. We must teach our children that it's serious business when we're dealing with our heavenly Father! We don't have to be frightened, but we do need to be honest and transparent before Him. Remember, He's not fooled by false words or hidden agendas.

Read Acts 5:1-11:
Ananias and Sapphira

But there was a certain man named Ananias who, with his wife, Sapphira, sold some property. He brought part of the money to the apostles, claiming it was the full amount. With his wife's consent, he kept the rest.

Then Peter said, "Ananias, why have you let Satan fill your heart? You lied to the Holy Spirit, and you kept some of the money for yourself. The property was yours to sell or not sell, as you wished. And after selling it, the money was also yours to give away. How could you do a thing like this? You weren't lying to us but to God!"

As soon as Ananias heard these words, he fell to the floor and died. Everyone who heard about it was terrified. Then some young men got up, wrapped him in a sheet, and took him out and buried him.

About three hours later his wife came in, not knowing what had happened. Peter asked her, "Was this the price you and your husband received for your land?"

"Yes," she replied, "that was the price."

And Peter said, "How could the two of you even think of conspiring to test the Spirit of the Lord like this? The young men who buried your husband are just outside the door, and they will carry you out, too."

Instantly, she fell to the floor and died. When the young men came in and saw that she was dead, they carried her out and buried her beside her husband. Great fear gripped the entire church and everyone else who heard what had happened.

Discussion Questions:

1. **Who were the main characters in this story?**
   Peter, Ananias and his wife, Sapphira

2. **What did Ananias and Sapphira do that was wrong?**
   They lied to the Holy Spirit.

3. **Was it wrong to sell their property and save the money?**
   No, the wrong was in lying to God.

4. **How did Peter know they were lying?**
   The Holy Spirit led him to the truth.

5. **What were the consequences of their sins?**

Both Ananias and Sapphira died.

6. What was the result in the Church in Acts?
Great fear gripped the entire church.

7. Why were they fearful?
They realized that God is powerful and that He knows what is in the hearts and minds of people; or God talks to His people!

8. What should we learn from this?
Answers will vary, but could include:

1. Honesty is very important to God.
2. We can't trick the Holy Spirit.

Notes: _____

_____

_____

_____

_____

_____

_____

_____

_____

_____

_____

_____

_____

_____

_____

_____

_____

_____

_____

_____

_____

_____

DAY 2: READ-ALOUD

THE WITNESS ZONE: "FRIENDS IN TOUGH PLACES"

Suggested Time: 15 minutes

Memory Verse: Trust in the Lord with all your heart, do not depend on your own understanding. Seek His will in all you do, and He will show you which path to take. —Proverbs 3:5-6

Lesson Instructions:

You are about to enter a zone unlike any other, where normal life becomes anything but normal and everyday conversations go from ordinary to shocking in the blink of an eye. It's a place where eternal choices are made, where faith meets fear and boldness meets hesitation. It is a zone where Superkids can become history-makers or bolt like a runaway train. Buckle your seat belts, and hold on for the ride. You are about to enter... "The Witness Zone."

There's one of your good friends. We'll call him Parker. He's sitting on the curb, staring at the ground. You sit down beside him.

"Hey, are you OK?" you ask.

Parker shrugs.

"Well," you say, "you're not acting like yourself today. Did someone eat your favorite cereal this morning?"

But Parker doesn't laugh. He just scrapes the ground with his foot. "My grandpa had to go to the hospital last night."

You pause for a moment. Then, "What's wrong with him?"

"They found out he has cancer." Parker sighs. "They say he might even die. The thought of my grandpa dying really scares me."

You fidget for a moment, not sure what to say. You reach into your pocket and pull out a yo-yo. "Wanna play with a yo-yo?"

Parker just shakes his head.

(Discuss what your children think about how the child in the lesson responded. What do they think about the situation? How would they have handled it? What do they think he should have said?)

Well, that was one way to handle it. There's your friend in need, definitely in a very tough place. But instead of helping, you got nervous and changed the subject...and "The Witness Zone" door slammed shut. But, all is not lost. Let's see what happens when you trust the Holy Spirit for just the right words instead. Let's read the story again, but this time change the ending.

Alternate Ending:

There's one of your good friends. We'll call him Parker. He's sitting on the curb, staring at the ground. You sit down beside him.

"Hey, are you OK?" you ask.

Parker shrugs.

"Well," you say, "you're not acting like yourself today. Did someone eat your favorite cereal this morning?"

But Parker doesn't laugh. He just scrapes the ground with his foot. "My grandpa had to go to the hospital last night."

You pause for a moment. Then, "What's wrong with him?"

"They found out he has cancer." Parker sighs. "They say he might even die. The thought of my grandpa dying really scares me."

You fidget for a moment, not sure what to say. You reach into your pocket, but then stop and ask the Holy Spirit to give you the right thing to say. You open your mouth and out come the words, "You know, your grandpa doesn't have to die."

Parker looks up. "What?"

You continue, "Well, Jesus came so that we could all have life. He wants us to have happy and healthy lives. He cares about you and your grandpa."

Parker scratches his head. "How do you know He cares about *us?*"

"Because," you explain, "He left heaven to die for you so you and your grandpa could be healed."

Parker takes a big breath. "Let me get this straight. You're saying that Jesus came all the way from heaven to die for us? And He can make my grandpa well?"

You nod. "That's what I'm saying."

"That's awesome!" Parker shouts. "Hey, we're going to the hospital later tonight! Can you come with us and tell my grandpa about that?"

"Of course!"

There you have it. One story, two different endings. Another opened door, another victory. A challenge given, and a challenge met. When you obey the Holy Spirit and tell Parker the good news of Jesus, Grandpa gets healed and Parker's entire family is changed! And, you learn to trust the Holy Spirit's lead even more. It's a zone that challenges every Superkid to ask this question: "What will I do next time I enter...'The Witness Zone'?"

Discussion Questions:

Enjoy these conversation starters with your children.

1. **Have you ever experienced a time when you felt the Holy Spirit telling you to say or do something? Tell me about it.**

2. **Have you ever had a time when someone was sad and you didn't know what to say? How did you handle it?**

3. **Do you wish you had handled it differently? If so, how?**

4. **Parents, share a time when you heard the Holy Spirit speaking to you. How did you know it was the Holy Spirit? What did His voice sound like?**

Notes: _____

_____

_____

_____

DAY 3: GIVING LESSON

PITCHING IN

Suggested Time: 10 minutes

Offering Scripture: They sold their property and possessions and shared the money with those in need.
—Acts 2:45

Supplies: ☐ Ready-made pudding cup, ☐ 1 Box "kid-friendly" cereal, ☐ 1 Juice box, ☐ 1 Clear glass, ☐ 1 Drinking straw, More items for additional children

Prior to Lesson:

Set up the kitchen table for a meal according to how many children you have participating. Place the pudding cup on the table in front of one of the chairs, at the next, place a box of cereal, at another, the juice box, at the next, the empty glass with the drinking straw, and so on, until each child's place has an item placed on the table in front of their chair.

Lesson Instructions:

Kids, you might notice some yummy snacks with me today. I wonder if any of you might be just a little bit hungry?

Invite children to sit at the table. *(Adjust your items to include the number of children in your group unless you have a large group. If your group is large, use three helpers.)*

OK, go ahead and enjoy the snacks that I brought for you. *(Wait for reaction from the kids. They should begin letting you know there are things they need in order for them to eat. Talk to each one and find out what it is they're missing—pudding: spoon; cereal: bowl and spoon; glass: something to drink, etc.)*

Actually, I was testing you today. You weren't able to enjoy your snacks properly because each of you was missing something you needed, weren't you?

Let me tell you a story about a group of people in the Bible that made sure every person in their church had what *they* needed.

In Acts 2, it says Peter went out in the street on the day the Holy Ghost came to the upper room, and started preaching. When he had finished preaching, 3,000 people asked Jesus into their hearts.

Guess what happened next? That group of people began sharing their dinner with each other and praying together every day. The Bible even says they would sell things and put their money together to help one another. God made sure everyone had what they needed. Isn't that amazing? People were loving each other so much that they partnered with God, watching to make sure people had what they needed. I don't know about you, but I want to be like those people in the book of Acts, and we can start by preparing an offering today.

What can we give that will show we are partnering with God to achieve His purposes on the earth? *(Allow kids to help choose how and what to give!)*

DAY 4: FOOD FUN

DIP INTO THE HOLY SPIRIT

Suggested Time: 10 minutes

Key Scripture: And the Holy Spirit helps us in our weakness. For example, we don't know what God wants us to pray for. But the Holy Spirit prays for us with groanings that cannot be expressed in words.—Romans 8:26

Teacher Tip: It would be a good idea to measure out all your ingredients ahead of time, but it's not vital. It's always fun to let kids assist by adding ingredients or stirring and, of course, you will need taste-testers. Don't forget to give the dip a few minutes to cool so you don't have any burnt tongues!

Popeye's® Favorite Dip Recipe:

Ingredients: ☐ 1 Minced garlic clove, ☐ 1/2 Cup mayonnaise, ☐ 1 Cup sour cream, ☐ 3/4 Cup canned artichoke hearts, chopped, ☐ 1/4 Cup chopped green chilies, ☐ 1 10-Ounce package of frozen chopped spinach (thaw, thoroughly drain, and squeeze out all excess water), ☐ 3/4 Cup parmesan cheese, ☐ 1/8 Teaspoon paprika, ☐ Cooking spray, ☐ 1 Package of pita bread (cut into wedges) or crackers

1. Spray a medium bowl with the cooking spray. Add garlic.
2. Cover tightly with plastic wrap and cook on high in microwave oven for 1 minute, or until the garlic sizzles.
3. Mix in the sour cream and mayonnaise.
4. Add all remaining dip ingredients to the sour cream mixture.
5. Cover with plastic wrap and heat in the microwave for 4-6 minutes, or until hot. Don't forget to use potholders when you take the bowl out of the microwave—it will be hot!
6. Serve with pita wedges or crackers. Yummy!

Supplies: ☐ Microwave oven, ☐ Medium-sized glass bowl, ☐ Large mixing spoon, ☐ Microwave-safe plastic wrap, ☐ Potholders, ☐ YouTube® clip of a Popeye® cartoon

Prior to Lesson:

Show a YouTube® clip of Popeye the Sailor Man® so that the kids will be familiar with the cartoon and the fact that Popeye® loves spinach!

Lesson Instructions:

Cooking with you is super-fun!

I like to call this special dip we are making today "Popeye's® Favorite." Can anyone guess why? It's because it has spinach in it. *(Follow recipe. Make sure you are the only one to handle the bowl when removing it from the microwave.)*

Now that we've completed making our yummy dip, would you like to give it a try?

In the Popeye® cartoons, what is the big deal about spinach? What supposedly happens to Popeye® when he rips open the can and pours the spinach into his mouth?

That's right, he immediately gets strong! Did you know that there is something we have as Christians that makes us extra strong? In Romans 8, it says the Holy Spirit helps us when we are weak. You could say He's kind of like our spinach, and when we connect with Him, we become superstrong in our spirits. How exciting is that? We can be stronger than Popeye®, and we don't even have to eat spinach (even though it's delicious and good for us!)

Notes: _____

_____

_____

_____

_____

_____

_____

_____

_____

_____

_____

_____

_____

_____

_____

_____

_____

_____

_____

_____

_____

_____

_____

_____

_____

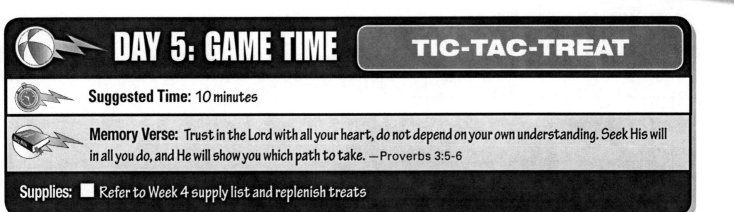

DAY 5: GAME TIME — TIC-TAC-TREAT

Suggested Time: 10 minutes

Memory Verse: Trust in the Lord with all your heart, do not depend on your own understanding. Seek His will in all you do, and He will show you which path to take. —Proverbs 3:5-6

Supplies: ■ Refer to Week 4 supply list and replenish treats

Game Instructions:

Refer to Week 4 game instructions and variations.

Game Goal:

Pay close attention to God's Word for opportunities to be blessed!

Final Word:

When we pay close attention to God's Word there are lots of awesome "treats" waiting for us, even better than "Tic-Tac-Treats"!

Refer to Week 4 for Tic-Tac-Treat letters to copy (X's and O's).

Notes: _____

_____

_____

_____

_____

_____

_____

_____

_____

_____

_____

TIC-TAC-TREAT QUESTIONS: VOL. 4/WEEK 7

(Review Taken From Vol. 4/Week 6)

BIBLE LESSON:

#1 <u>Question:</u> <u>Who asks us to honor and respect authority?</u>
Answer: God.

#2 <u>Question:</u> <u>What are we supposed to do for our leaders?</u>
Answer: Pray for them.

#3 <u>Question:</u> <u>Why does God want us to pray for our leaders?</u>
Answer: He wants everyone to be saved; or He wants us to live quiet and peaceable lives.

#4 <u>Question:</u> <u>When we honor our leaders, who else are we honoring?</u>
Answer: God.

#5 <u>Question:</u> What does God promise us when we honor our leaders?
Answer: Peace and quiet/"The Sweet Life."

GIVING LESSON:

#6 <u>Question:</u> <u>Where should you decide how much you will give to God?</u>
Answer: In your heart.

#7 <u>Question:</u> <u>Where should you not decide how much you will give?</u>
Answer: In your head.

MEMORY VERSE:

#8 <u>Question:</u> <u>What was last week's memory verse?</u>
Answer: "Everyone must submit to governing authorities. For all authority comes from God, and those in positions of authority have been placed there by God." Romans 13:1

OBJECT LESSON:

#9 <u>Question:</u> <u>List four different leaders we learned we should honor.</u>
Answer: Teacher, pastor, police, president.

READ-ALOUD:

#10 <u>Question:</u> <u>How did Lexie help her angry Sunday school teacher?</u>
Answer: She prayer for her, and then helped her sort papers.

TIC-TAC-TREAT (10 QUESTIONS TOTAL)

BIBLE LESSON: (5 questions)

#1 Q: _____

_____

A: _____

_____

#2 Q: _____

_____

A: _____

_____

#3 Q: _____

_____

A: _____

_____

#4 Q: _____

_____

A: _____

_____

#5 Q: _____

_____

A: _____

_____

Notes: _____

_____

_____

TIC-TAC-TREAT (10 QUESTIONS TOTAL)

GIVING LESSON: (2 questions)

#1 Q:_____

_____

A:_____

_____

#2 Q:_____

_____

A:_____

_____

MEMORY VERSE: (1 question)

#1 Q:_____

_____

A:_____

_____

WILD CARD: (2 questions)

#1 Q:_____

_____

A:_____

_____

#2 Q:_____

_____

A:_____

_____

ACTIVITY PAGE

JERUSALEM MARKETPLACE LOOK-AND-FIND

Memory Verse: Trust in the Lord with all your heart, do not depend on your own understanding. Seek His will in all you do, and He will show you which path to take. —Proverbs 3:5-6

This week you've learned the importance of seeking the Lord's will in all you do. You want to tune in to the Holy Spirit—listening to and obeying all He tells you to do.

Today, see how well your earthly "seekers" (your eyes) are working. Find these 10 items: a rake, a birthday hat, a whistle, a Bible, a cereal box, a milk jug, a sheep with black spots, a boot, a lunchbox and a ladder.

ANSWER KEY

Notes: _____

_____

_____

_____

_____

_____

_____

_____

_____

_____

_____

Series: The Heart of a Superkid

WEEK 8: GREATNESS GOD'S WAY

WEEK 8

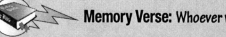 **Memory Verse:** *Whoever wants to be first must take last place and be the servant of everyone else.*—Mark 9:35b

WEEK 8: SNAPSHOT

GREATNESS GOD'S WAY

DAY	TYPE OF LESSON	LESSON TITLE	SUPPLIES
Day 1	Bible Lesson	Who Is the Greatest?	None
Day 2	Storybook Theater	Greatness	Whiteboard or chalkboard or easel with paper, Markers or pastel chalks, Rags (to blend chalks), Pencil and eraser (art pencils work best, **Optional costumes/props:** Jeans, T-shirt, Hand-held video game (for Marcel), Shorts, T-shirt, Sandbox toys (for Sam), Large, well-worn Bible (for Mom)
Day 3	Giving Lesson	Whistle While You Work?	Whiteboard, Dry-erase markers, Whiteboard eraser
Day 4	Object Lesson	Secret Servants	Small notepads or paper for lists, Pencils or pens
Day 5	Game Time	Serve's Up!	2 Round waiter-style trays filled with "nonspillable" food-related items, 2 Server aprons
Bonus	Activity Page	How Many Words?	1 Copy for each child

Lesson Introduction:

We, as leaders (parents and teachers), must learn this one truth: Greatness is coming as surely as the sun rises. May I ask you a couple of questions?

- Do you feel important when people make a big deal over you?

- Do you enjoy when your opinion obviously matters to someone?

Here is what really counts: If you as a leader in your home will serve your children and your spouse or other family members, you will be great in God's eyes. It doesn't matter whether people applaud or give you the credit for your ministry. It doesn't even matter if they notice or not! What counts is what Jesus said in Mark 9. Be a servant and you are great. Try to be important and you're just another noisemaker. Let's allow God to make us great HIS way!

Commander Dana
Commander Dana

Lesson Outline:

This week you'll be focusing your study on servant leadership. What a wonderful concept to emphasize within your home! It's so powerful for your children to see you serving the family, not grudgingly, but joyfully because of your love for them. They will thrive in the loving environment and ultimately see you following after Jesus with a servant's heart.

I. JESUS' DISCIPLES WANTED TO BE GREAT

a. They had seen many amazing and wonderful miracles.

b. Jesus explained mysteries about God to them. Mark 4:10-11

c. The disciples felt very special being so close to Jesus.

d. Sometimes, even people who are close to the Lord start to think they are more important than others.

II. GOD WANTS US TO DO GREAT THINGS

a. He loves it when we use our faith. Using faith is great! Hebrews 11:6

b. Jesus said we could heal sick people. Healing is great, too! Mark 16:18

c. The disciples began to argue about which of them was the greatest. Mark 9:33-34

III. JESUS EXPLAINS THE TRUTH ABOUT GREATNESS Mark 9:35

a. The world says someone is great if lots of people serve him or her.

b. Jesus says that a really great person is one who serves everyone else.

c. To be a great person in God's eyes, don't try to get people to serve you. Instead, try to see how many people you can serve. That's what Jesus did!

Notes:_____

_____

_____

_____

_____

_____

_____

_____

DAY 1: BIBLE LESSON

WHO IS THE GREATEST?

Memory Verse: *Whoever wants to be first must take last place and be the servant of everyone else.*
—Mark 9:35b

Today, you'll be introducing the idea of servant leadership within your family. You probably know areas where your family members could improve, but allow the Holy Spirit to speak to you and your children and see what amazing things God will do as He works on the hearts of those in your family.

Read Mark 9:33-37:
Who Is the Greatest?

After they arrived at Capernaum and settled in a house, Jesus asked his disciples, "What were you discussing out on the road?"

But they didn't answer, because they had been arguing about which of them was the greatest.

He sat down, called the twelve disciples over to him, and said, "Whoever wants to be first must take last place and be the servant of everyone else."

Then he put a little child among them. Taking the child in his arms, he said to them, "Anyone who welcomes a little child like this on my behalf welcomes me, and anyone who welcomes me welcomes not only me but also my Father who sent me."

Discussion Questions:

1. **Why do you think the disciples didn't want to answer Jesus' question about what they were discussing?**
   Because they were embarrassed to admit they were fighting about who was the best!

2. **How did Jesus respond?**
   He calmly sat down and called everybody together.

3. **How do you think this made the disciples feel who were arguing?**
   Answers will vary, but most likely they felt embarrassed and ashamed of their bragging!

4. **What did Jesus say was the secret to greatness?**
   He said to become a servant and then you will be great.

5. **Do you think this comes naturally to most people?**
   No!

6. **Whom did Jesus say we should serve?**
   He recommended serving kids! He said God would be pleased (Verse 37)!

7. **Who do you find it difficult to serve?**
   Answers will vary.

8. **Who will you decide to serve with a joyful heart?**
   Allow kids to brainstorm who and how to serve.

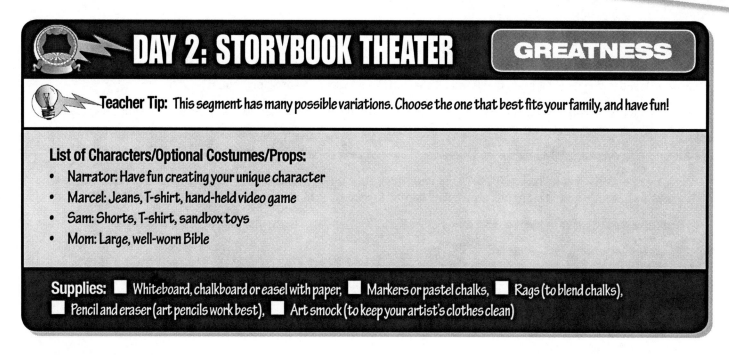

DAY 2: STORYBOOK THEATER

GREATNESS

Teacher Tip: This segment has many possible variations. Choose the one that best fits your family, and have fun!

List of Characters/Optional Costumes/Props:
- Narrator: Have fun creating your unique character
- Marcel: Jeans, T-shirt, hand-held video game
- Sam: Shorts, T-shirt, sandbox toys
- Mom: Large, well-worn Bible

Supplies: ■ Whiteboard, chalkboard or easel with paper, ■ Markers or pastel chalks, ■ Rags (to blend chalks), ■ Pencil and eraser (art pencils work best), ■ Art smock (to keep your artist's clothes clean)

Variation No. 1:

Read the story as part of your read-aloud time.

Variation No. 2:

Read the story like an old-time radio skit, complete with different actors for each part. If you are limited on participants, then allow more than one part per person and change the voice. Make copies of the skit, and have each actor highlight their lines.

Variation No. 3:

Act out the story as a fun skit. Perhaps your children can practice during the day (even creating fun costumes from everyday items) and then perform it in the evening before the whole family. Before beginning your skit, remember to introduce your cast!

Variation No. 4:

Create a storybook theater where one or more family members sketch the story on a whiteboard, chalkboard or artist's easel, as another member reads the story. Initially, there will be a few supplies to purchase, but don't let this be a deterrent from using the illustrated story option! Once the supplies have been purchased, they'll be long-lasting and reusable. Teacher tip: Cut the paper to fit on the board and tape it down. Lightly sketch the drawing with a pencil prior to presentation. Time may not allow for the picture to be completely drawn and colored during the story. Erase the pencil lines, so light lines are visible to you but not to your audience. Review the story ahead of time to determine the amount of time needed to complete the illustration while telling the story. When the story begins, use black markers to draw the picture, tracing your pencil lines. Next, apply color using the pastel chalk. Then, blend the color with the rags to complete the picture.

Story:

Marcel loved to do lots of different things, and it seemed like he was good at all of them.

His favorite saying whenever he did something cool was "Greatness!" For instance, if Marcel was playing basketball and made a three-pointer, he would smile and say, "Greatness!"

Anyone who was around Marcel for very long would hear that word spoken quite a bit.

Now, there was one thing Marcel did NOT enjoy very much, and it was taking care of his kid brother. Sam was only 3, and constantly pestered his older brother. Sam called him "Cel" instead of Marcel, probably because he was 3.

"Marcel, would you please help your brother pick up his stuff?" he heard his mother ask from the hallway.

"I'm sort of busy, Mom," he answered.

Marcel was playing his favorite video game, called "Invisible Cockroaches From Space." Marcel aimed his laser pointer and nailed the remaining enemy cockroaches.

"Greatness!" he exclaimed.

"What was that, dear?" Mom said.

"Just the usual, Mom," Marcel answered, as his mother picked up Sam's clothes from the floor.

"Can you please take Sam to the backyard and play in the sandbox with him for a while?"

Marcel didn't like the sandbox at all. There was nothing to win there, so what was fun about that? Besides, sometimes the sand got wet and stuck to your clothes.

Sam walked toward his brother and said, "Box!"

Marcel made a face, and tossed his laser controller toward the shelf that he kept his game stuff on. The weapon landed on the shelf and slid to a stop against the stack of games right where it belonged.

"Greatness!" proclaimed Marcel.

As Sam played in the sandbox, Marcel frowned.

"Why does Mom make me watch this.....baby?" he wondered, as Sam happily made a pile of sand, placing a plastic cup on top. Sam smiled.

"C'mon, Cel," Sam shouted. "We have fun!"

Marcel looked disgusted and opened the door.

"Mom, I can't stand the sandbox anymore," he shouted. "Sam wants to come in now."

His mother waved them in. Sam was not happy about leaving his sand pile. He protested as Marcel lifted him out of the sand.

"We play sand, Cel, we play sand!"

Ignoring his brother's crying, Marcel said, "Mom wants you to come in, and I can't do anything about it."

As they came through the door, Marcel picked up an orange that had rolled off the table. He tossed it behind his back. Thump! It landed in the basket of fruit and wobbled to a stop.

"Greatness!" he said, walking into his room and shutting the door as Sam wailed in the living room.

After dinner, Marcel's mom washed the dishes while her older son attacked unseen space cockroaches in the other room.

Every few minutes she would hear him say "Greatness!" After Sam had been put to bed, Marcel's mom asked him to sit with her for a few minutes. She held her Bible in her lap and opened it.

"Son," she started, "I'm glad you like to do things that have 'greatness' in them. In fact, it's your favorite saying as far as I can tell." Marcel looked at his mom and grinned.

"I guess I do say that a lot," he answered.

Mom continued. "Well, you may not realize it, but God has a big appreciation for greatness too."

She opened her old Bible, which she had read for years.

"Listen to what God's Word says about wanting to be the greatest."

His mother cleared her throat and began to read.

"A controversy arose among them as to which of them should be the greatest. But Jesus took a little child and put him at His side and said, Whoever wants to be the greatest should be a servant. And whoever welcomes a little child on my behalf welcomes me also."

She closed the book and looked at her son.

"Greatness God's way is always being unselfish. Greatness God's way is being a blessing to others. God wants you to be great—but He says greatness is what we do for other people."

Later that night, Marcel climbed into bed and yawned. As he lay down, he felt something jab him in the side. Digging around under his covers he pulled out a walkie-talkie that had been missing for a week.

"Where have you been hiding?" asked Marcel as he flung it toward the dresser. The walkie-talkie bounced off the back wall, bumped into the lamp and wobbled to a stop, standing up perfectly, right next to the battery charger. Marcel smiled sleepily but didn't say anything.

The next morning Marcel woke up with Sam's face about 2 inches from his. Sam was standing next to Marcel's bed holding a toy rocket.

"We play rock?" Sam asked.

Marcel started to tell Sam to leave him alone, but before he spoke, he remembered what Mom had read to him the night before. Marcel heard strange words coming out of his mouth.

"Sure, little man," he said. "We can play rocket in the sandbox if you want."

Sam smiled and shouted, "Sand!"

Marcel changed into his jeans and went out to the sandbox. He helped Sam build a launch pad for the rocket, and together they 'blasted off' about 50 times. Sam was tireless in the sandbox. Marcel's mother watched from the kitchen window. Her older son was helping his kid brother have fun in the somewhat-wet sandbox.

"Greatness!" she said.

(Story by Dana Johnson)

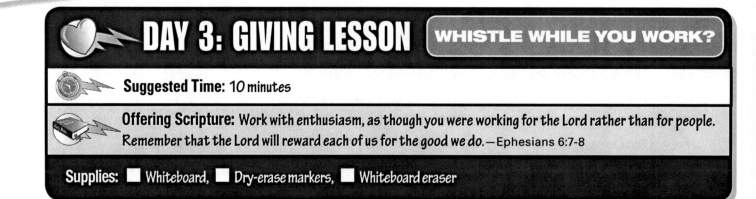

DAY 3: GIVING LESSON — WHISTLE WHILE YOU WORK?

Suggested Time: 10 minutes

Offering Scripture: Work with enthusiasm, as though you were working for the Lord rather than for people. Remember that the Lord will reward each of us for the good we do. —Ephesians 6:7-8

Supplies: ■ Whiteboard, ■ Dry-erase markers, ■ Whiteboard eraser

Lesson Instructions:

Are you ready to teach today?

You may be thinking, "Wait a minute, you're the one who's supposed to be teaching us!" Well, there's a verse I would like to read to you, and then I will need your help. We are going to think of some ideas on how we can actually do what this scripture is telling us.

Here's our verse from Ephesians 6:7-8, "Work with enthusiasm, as though you were working for the Lord rather than for people. Remember that the Lord will reward each of us for the good we do."

God's Word tells us that we are supposed to work with enthusiasm. That means we are to be happy and excited to be working. It also says we are to work like we're working for the Lord. Does that mean all of you need to go and get a job preaching, or maybe get a TV show so you can teach God's Word?

No, I think it's talking about a different kind of work. Perhaps something we can do right here.

You may have noticed this board. It's for writing a list of things we could do that would be "working for the Lord." Let's see what our list looks like when we are finished. *(Lead the children to think of ideas for things they could put their hands to like: take out the trash, feed the dog, clean out the bathroom, sweep or vacuum, help an elderly neighbor with yardwork or chores, babysit someone's child, etc.)*

It's so exciting to see that there are all kinds of things we can do for God, and you don't even have to be a grown-up to do them. And remember, God says He will reward each of you for the good you do. What kind of rewards? Oh, just stick around and see: His rewards are amazing!

You know, one way we can work for the Lord right now is to bring Him our tithes and offerings. Let's be the happy, enthusiastic givers who God rewards as we prepare our offering for church. And then, let's give an offering of time by choosing one or more of the activities we wrote on the board to do this week!

Notes: _____

_____

_____

_____

_____

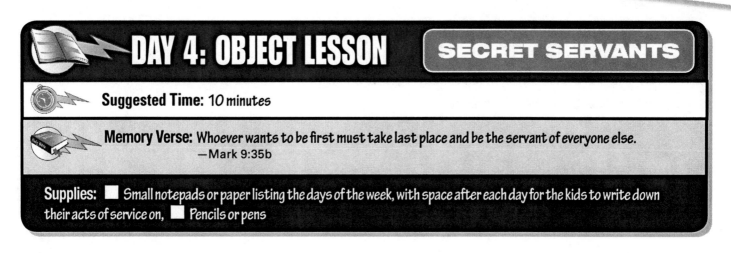

DAY 4: OBJECT LESSON — SECRET SERVANTS

Suggested Time: 10 minutes

Memory Verse: Whoever wants to be first must take last place and be the servant of everyone else.
—Mark 9:35b

Supplies: ☐ Small notepads or paper listing the days of the week, with space after each day for the kids to write down their acts of service on, ☐ Pencils or pens

Lesson Instructions:

How many of you have ever thought it would be cool to be a secret agent? Well, guess what? This coming week you are actually going to get a chance to see just how good you are at being mysterious! You're probably wondering what in the world I'm talking about. Let me explain.

Do you remember in Mark 9 the conversation Jesus had with His disciples? The disciples had been talking between themselves about who was the best disciple—who was the greatest. You know, some people think that to be great you have to be a supermodel or a sports star. Even back in Jesus' day people wanted to be popular and looked up to. But Jesus let the disciples know they were thinking all wrong. He said to be great, you must be a servant.

Now, back to the secret agent thing. I have a very special assignment for you. For the next week, you are to choose one person who you will do something special for every day. I'll even give you some ideas to get started. You could leave him or her an encouraging note, give a little gift or find a scripture, write it out and put it where the person can find it. You will need to be creative and come up with fun things to do each day of the week.

Now, here's the catch: YOU MUST KEEP YOUR IDENTITY A SECRET!

I will be handing out special papers for you to record what you do every day. Be sure and bring your list of "secret serving" back with you next week, and remember, it's TOP SECRET!

Jesus said, "Whoever wants to be first must take last place and be the servant of everyone else." Did He go around calling attention to Himself and making sure everyone noticed the good things He was doing? No, of course not. You might even say Jesus was a secret agent of doing good.

What do you think, kids? Are you up for this challenge—are you ready to get a little sneaky and become a secret servant for God?

Notes: _____

_____

_____

_____

_____

DAY 5: GAME TIME — SERVE'S UP!

Suggested Time: 7-10 minutes

Memory Verse: Whoever wants to be first must take last place and be the servant of everyone else. —Mark 9:35b

Supplies: ■ 2 Round, waiter-style trays filled with "nonspillable" food-related items, ■ 2 Server aprons

Prior to Game:

Teach all the children the memory verse. Have the first kids put on the apron and hold the trays head-high, waiter style.

Game Instructions:

Instruct your "waiters" to prepare their trays, and then have them say the verse. As soon as they correctly quote the verse, they must walk around the room (or through a pre-set course of your design) trying not to spill any items from the tray. If they spill, they must pick up the dropped item and say the memory verse again while standing still. After repeating the verse, they may start moving again.

Once they successfully make it back to the front of the room, they give the apron and tray to the next team member, and so on.

Game Goal:

The fastest person to complete their "server training" wins.

Final Word:

After this game, tell your kids what great servers they are. Remember what Jesus said in Matthew 23:11, KJV: "But he that is greatest among you shall be your servant." Our goal should be to see how many people we can serve every day!

Variation No. 1: Individual Players

If your group is small, time each round and determine the winner, based on their individual speed. The sillier the items, the more fun the game can be. For example, a plastic egg, a spoon, a plastic cup, etc., will be harder to balance than a flat book.

Variation No. 2: Obstacle Course

To increase the difficulty of the game, add obstacles to your course. You may choose to add the obstacles at the beginning of the game or play a series of rounds to determine the Ultimate Winner. Just add an additional obstacle after each round. Players must complete the round successfully to move on to the next round. Continue until there is only one player left. Obstacles could include stepping over blocks or maneuvering around chairs or even bending down to go under a broomstick.

ACTIVITY PAGE — HOW MANY WORDS?

Memory Verse: Whoever wants to be first must take last place and be the servant of everyone else.
—Mark 9:35b

This week you've been learning about the real meaning of greatness. Today, use this sheet to find how many words (three letters or more) you can make out of the letters in the word GREATNESS. Try to find at least 30.

ANSWER KEY

This is not an exhaustive list. In fact, there are more than 400 words that can be made from the letters in the word GREAT-NESS, but these are some of the most common ones.

age	earn	gate	net	seat	steer
agent	earnest	gear	rag	see	stern
agree	ease	gene	rage	seen	strange
anger	east	genre	range	senate	tag
angst	eastern	get	rant	sense	tan
ant	eat	grant	rat	sent	tar
ante	eaten	grass	rate	serge	tea
are	eats	grate	regent	sergeant	tear
art	egret	grease	rent	set	ten
assent	enrage	great	resent	snag	tense
assert	enter	green	reset	snare	tree
asset	era	greet	rest	sneer	
aster	erase	near	sage	stag	
ate	estrange	nearest	sang	stage	
eager	garnet	neat	sat	star	
ear	gas	nest	sea	stare	

Notes: _____

_____

_____

_____

_____

_____

_____

_____

_____

_____

_____

_____

WEEK 9: SERVING YOUR NEIGHBOR

 Memory Verse: Honor your father and mother. Love your neighbor as yourself.—Matthew 19:19

WEEK 9: SNAPSHOT — SERVING YOUR NEIGHBOR

DAY	TYPE OF LESSON	LESSON TITLE	SUPPLIES
Day 1	Bible Lesson	Good Neighbors	None
Day 2	Food Fun	Dinner Is Served	Table service for each child, (plates, silverware, napkins, glasses), Cookies and milk for each child
Day 3	Giving Lesson	God to the Rescue!	Some kind of flotation device (an inner tube, pair of arm floats, etc.), Ladder or sheet, 1 or 2 Dollar bills, A loaf of bread, A kid's coat or jacket with a hood
Day 4	Real Deal	Mother Teresa	**Optional Costume:** Dress in some way like Mother Teresa
Day 5	Game Time	Fun Cereal Feed	2-4 Plastic spoons, 2-4 Small plastic-handled goldfish-type nets, 2 Bowls, 1 Box of breakfast cereal, 2 Chairs, Small prop table, Upbeat game music
Bonus	Activity Page	Good Neighbor Crossword	1 Copy for each child

Lesson Introduction:

One Sunday morning while teaching Children's Church, I announced we were going to start a Hospitality Team. This team would have a special room for getting to know first-time guests, and it would have its own snacks, games, etc. Every kid in the room was immediately attentive! I explained I needed leaders, and so for the next month, before selecting the team members, I would be watching closely every Sunday morning to see who was friendly and thoughtful. I had no clue what was about to happen from this one idea.

For the next month, the kids at our church displayed friendliness of tsunami proportions! It was almost comical when visitors would walk through the door! They would be surrounded by boys and girls offering to help them register. Next, the kids would introduce the newcomers to their friends, and then take them to a saved seat in the (coveted) front row. The spirit of neighborly servanthood was born!

This can apply to your home or neighborhood, too. Teach your children to serve those around them, and watch the warmth in relationships from the glow of hospitality and servanthood at work!

Commander Dana
Commander Dana

Lesson Outline:

This week, sit back and enjoy God at work in your family as you teach the wonderful concept of servant leadership within their community! You'll find plenty of practical examples and see that God will do amazing things as your kids grasp this vital concept.

I. GOD'S WORD COMMANDS US TO LOVE OUR NEIGHBOR

    a. God knows the needs of every person.

    b. Even small things are important to God. Matthew 10:42

    c. Our Father is depending on us to be servants!

II. A MAN DECIDED TO TRAVEL TO JERICHO Luke 10:30-35

    a. He was attacked by vicious thieves and left for dead.

    b. A priest saw him lying there and walked way around him.

    c. A Levite stared at him for a while and then walked away.

    d. A despised foreigner from Samaria stopped and saved his life.

III. WHAT A TRUE NEIGHBOR DOES

    a. A godly neighbor cares for those who are in trouble.

    b. A true neighbor will help someone who is hurt.

    c. Great neighbors will never leave someone lonely!

    d. It doesn't matter if we know them or not. What matters is, "Do they need my help?"

Notes:_____

_____

_____

_____

_____

_____

_____

_____

DAY 1: BIBLE LESSON — GOOD NEIGHBORS

Memory Verse: Honor your father and mother. Love your neighbor as yourself. —Matthew 19:19

This week, you'll be discussing how to be a good neighbor and serve others. Look for ways to encourage hospitality and servant leadership among your children. You'll be blessed, and they'll be excited to learn that serving God is full of variety!

Read Luke 10:30-37:
The Parable of the Good Samaritan

"A Jewish man was traveling from Jerusalem down to Jericho, and he was attacked by bandits. They stripped him of his clothes, beat him up, and left him half dead beside the road.

"By chance a priest came along. But when he saw the man lying there, he crossed to the other side of the road and passed him by. A Temple assistant walked over and looked at him lying there, but he also passed by on the other side.

"Then a despised Samaritan came along, and when he saw the man, he felt compassion for him. Going over to him, the Samaritan soothed his wounds with olive oil and wine and bandaged them. Then he put the man on his own donkey and took him to an inn, where he took care of him. The next day he handed the innkeeper two silver coins, telling him, 'Take care of this man. If his bill runs higher than this, I'll pay you the next time I'm here.'

"Now which of these three would you say was a neighbor to the man who was attacked by bandits?" Jesus asked.

The man replied, "The one who showed him mercy."

Then Jesus said, "Yes, now go and do the same."

Discussion Questions:

1. **Who was attacked?**
   A Jewish man who was traveling

2. **Name the three individuals who saw the man was injured.**
   The priest, the Temple assistant and the Samaritan

3. **Who stopped to help the man who was hurt?**
   The Samaritan

4. **What did he do?**
   He soothed the man's wounds, bandaged him and then took the man to a place to get well.

5. **Why do you think only one person of the three who saw the man stopped to help?**
   Answers will vary but accept reasonable, thoughtful responses.

6. **From this story, Jesus told His disciples to help those in need. Who is in need?**
   Those who are in need include the hungry, the poor, the hurting and the lonely.

7. Do you think it's always easy or convenient to help others? Why or why not?
No, it takes our time and energy, and sometimes it requires us to help people who are not easy to help or love.

8. Who are some people you might be able to help?
Allow time for kids to think of one or two practical applications to this story.

Notes: _____

_____

_____

_____

_____

_____

_____

_____

_____

_____

_____

_____

_____

_____

_____

_____

_____

_____

_____

_____

_____

_____

_____

_____

_____

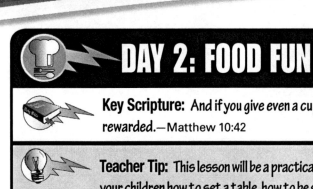

DAY 2: FOOD FUN

DINNER IS SERVED

Key Scripture: And if you give even a cup of cold water to one of the least of my followers, you will surely be rewarded.—Matthew 10:42

Teacher Tip: This lesson will be a practical application in learning how to serve one another. You will be teaching your children how to set a table, how to be seated and how to conduct themselves at mealtimes—all things that will be a blessing to your family.

Supplies: ☐ Table service for each child in your family (plates, silverware, napkins, glasses), ☐ Cookies and milk for each child

Lesson Instructions:

Since we're learning about being servants, I thought it would be fun to see if you know how to do some things that servants used to do for their masters a long time ago. The first test has to do with setting the table. *(Have the table service stacked up and placed in the center of the table.)*

Who would like to show us how to set the table?

(A refresher: knife and spoon to the right of the plate, with knife on the inside, cutting edge facing toward the plate and spoon on the outside; fork on the left side on top of the neatly folded napkin; glass on right side of plate near the tip of the knife.)

Let's see how you did. *(Walk them through any corrections needed, making sure to focus on the parts they did well.)*

Now that we have the table set, let's add a little snack and do one more test! *(Place the cookies on the plates and pour milk into the glasses.)*

(Invite your children to be seated and have a snack. More than likely, they will just sit down and start eating. This is your opportunity to teach them some dinnertime etiquette. Have the boy pull out the chair for the girl, and help her get seated. Remind them to place their napkins in their laps and, of course, don't forget to pray! If there is no boy in your group, you can have someone pretend to be the boy so that they each get turns.)

Did you know that Jesus talked a lot about being a servant? Why do you think that is such a big deal to the Lord?

Because He knows that when we do things for others, when we put others before ourselves, we are acting just like God.

Just think of it this way—when you set the table and "mind your manners" at dinnertime, you are being a blessing to your family. You are being like the servant whose first thought is how he can help the ones around him. And that's a big deal to God!

Note: This is a great opportunity to teach your children to serve through hospitality! Enjoy these other options as you make a fun family memory.

Variation No. 1:

Make this a family event for dinner. In addition to setting the table (possibly using your nice china), children can pull out tablecloths and cloth napkins. They can also put their artistic talents to work by making a festive centerpiece.

Variations No. 2:

If you have young girls, consider planning a "tea party." Give each girl a turn as "hostess." Allow her to welcome her guests, pour the tea and serve the treats.

Variations No. 3:

If your family is all boys, consider having them role-play dad for the evening. They can pull out mom's chair, sit at the head of the table, tell the family about their day and ask the other family members about theirs.

Variations No. 4:

Coordinate a real dinner party with another family. Allow the kids to prepare the table and serve the meal. Remember to keep the menu simple so that they can be successful and safe.

Notes: _____

_____

_____

_____

_____

_____

_____

_____

_____

_____

_____

_____

_____

_____

_____

_____

_____

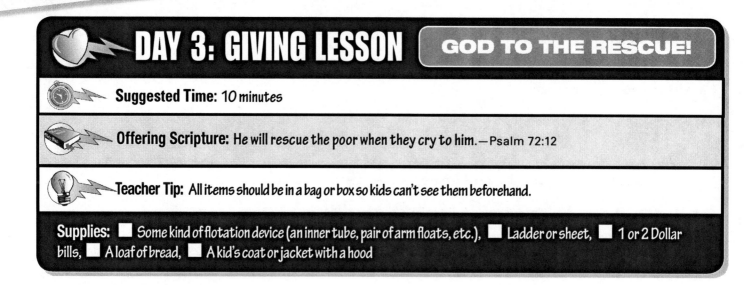

DAY 3: GIVING LESSON — GOD TO THE RESCUE!

Suggested Time: 10 minutes

Offering Scripture: He will rescue the poor when they cry to him. —Psalm 72:12

Teacher Tip: All items should be in a bag or box so kids can't see them beforehand.

Supplies: ☐ Some kind of flotation device (an inner tube, pair of arm floats, etc.), ☐ Ladder or sheet, ☐ 1 or 2 Dollar bills, ☐ A loaf of bread, ☐ A kid's coat or jacket with a hood

Lesson Instructions:

Can you give me an example of a hero? *(Get input from the kids, whether fictitious or real characters.)*

I have a few things with me today that certain kinds of heroes use. Maybe you can help me figure out who they are.

In my hands, I have something you all are probably familiar with: a pair of arm floats for swimming! What hero would use these? *(You may not get the correct response on this.)*

A lifeguard? Yes. Of course, a real lifeguard would probably need something a little bigger than arm floats for swimming if he were trying to save someone from drowning.

Let's move on to our next hero. I have this big bedsheet. What hero would need a big sheet? *(Accept a few more guesses.)*

A fireman, of course! Have you ever seen those movies where buildings are on fire and people are jumping out of windows onto what looks like a sheet, while the firemen hold the edges? Well, it isn't really a sheet, but it looks sort of like one!

There's one thing these two heroes have in common—they're rescuers. They come to the rescue of people who are in serious trouble and need the help of someone who knows what to do. Did you know there's a verse in Psalms which talks about a rescuer? It's in Psalm 72:12: "He will rescue the poor."

Wow, that verse says that God is a rescuer of the poor and—check this part out—He doesn't wait around until they're starving and have nothing to wear. It says He rescues them when they cry to Him.

Now, I have a few more things to show you, but first I want to see if anyone can tell me what things a "rescuer of the poor" might have?

(Get a few answers from the kids. You may have to help them get started, but it would be best if they initiate ideas.)

Think about it—a rescuer of the poor might need some money *(show the dollar bills)* or some food *(show the bread)* or maybe even some clothes *(show the coat).*

How do you think God actually rescues the poor? How does He get these things to the people who need them?

He uses *people* like you and me who will listen to His voice and do what He asks them to do. We can also help rescue others by bringing our offerings to church! Many times, the money we give helps buy things for people who are hungry, need clothes or maybe even need a place to stay. Do you want to be a "rescuer for God"? Let's get started in our first rescue mission by bringing our offerings to the Lord. We can prepare our offering now for Sunday!

Notes: _____

_____

_____

_____

_____

_____

_____

_____

_____

_____

_____

_____

_____

_____

_____

_____

_____

_____

_____

_____

_____

_____

_____

_____

_____

_____

_____

_____

_____

_____

_____

_____

_____

DAY 4: REAL DEAL

MOTHER TERESA

Memory Verse: *Honor your father and mother. Love your neighbor as yourself.*—Matthew 19:19

Concept: Highlighting an interesting historical place, figure or event that illustrates the theme of the day. The theme of the day is serving your neighbor.

Media: If you have the technical capability, show media photos of Mother Teresa ministering to the sick and poor. If you do not have this capability, you may print out photos from the Internet to show the kids or check out a book from your local library.

Teacher Tip: This segment has many possible variations. Choose the one that best fits your family, and have fun!

Optional Costume: ☐ Dress in some way like Mother Teresa (will lend to presentation interest).

Variation No. 1:

Entering in costume is an attention grabber for your children. When presenting the information, it's helpful to have pictures available. Check out books from the library or print pictures from the Internet of humanitarian efforts to meet the physical, social and spiritual needs of people throughout the world.

Variation No. 2:

Have your children dress up as Mother Teresa and re-enact some of what they have learned about her efforts to help people in obedience to God. This open-ended activity will produce the intrinsic awareness that servanthood involves each individual making a difference—one person at a time.

Variation No. 3:

If you are part of a home school co-op with teenagers involved, consider having a friend dress up as Mother Teresa for added dramatic flair.

Intro:

Today, we are talking about serving our neighbor. True servants help the hurting and lonely. No one has ever been a bigger or better servant than Jesus, but He's had some help from His servant heroes throughout history.

One servant in particular became famous for helping the poor, the hurting and lonely. This lady spent her entire life helping people no one else wanted to help, just like the Good Samaritan did in the Bible. She wasn't powerful or rich, but she certainly was strong in character and rich in love. First she impacted India, and then she started rescue missions for the poor, sick and dying all over the world.

She built homes for kids to live in who had no parents, and they called her "Mother." Any Superkid know who this mystery hero is?

Lesson Instructions:

About Agnes Bojaxhiu:

People called this amazing servant "Mother Teresa." But, way before she was "Mother Teresa," she was a kid just like you. As a kid, her name was Gonxha Agnes Bojaxhiu (Boh-yah-JOO). Try saying that last name all the time! Agnes was born in 1910 in Skopje, Macedonia, of Albanian parents. Any geography whizzes out there know where Macedonia is? It is a small country just north of Greece that used to be called Yugoslavia.

Agnes' family had been well-to-do until her father died when she was only 7[1], so money became tight, and her mother had to work very hard to support them. Even though there wasn't much money, there was plenty of love and faith in the Bojaxhiu home. This made it a great place to learn. One of Agnes' favorite things to do was read stories about missionaries who spent their lives serving others. When she was 12, Agnes was convinced that she too wanted to spend her life serving God and other people.

Road Trip…to India!:

By the time she was 18, Agnes wanted to go on a road trip. But this was no ordinary road trip to the beach or on vacation. This road trip was to Dublin, Ireland, to work with a missionary charity called the Sisters of Loreto[2] who helped and educated young girls. The following year, when she was 19, Agnes was sent by them to work as a missionary in India…all by herself! Can you imagine your parents letting you go to India by yourself? For years, Agnes had been dreaming of serving others. Now she finally was on her way.

No friends, no family—just her and her teammate Jesus.

For the next 17 years, she taught at a girls' school in Calcutta, India. That's what I call a long road trip! She eventually became the principal of the school and loved the children there[3]. Although she loved the children, God had other BIG plans for Agnes.

Road Trip…Part Two:

For some reason, big things seemed to start for Agnes on road trips. Agnes had become a nun, and had changed her named to "Teresa," after another servant who did big things for God. This time, Teresa had set out on a "get well" trip. After all her hard work, she had gotten sick and needed some time to recover. Little did she know that her "get well" trip would really be a "get busy" trip!

On the train ride, the Lord spoke to Teresa and told her she had a BIG call to take care of the sick, dying, hungry and homeless. He wanted her to be His love in action to the poorest of the poor. The greatest calling of all—a servant! That's when Teresa made a decision to leave her good job as a teacher, and bravely reach out to the unwanted and unloved.

[1] "Who Was Blessed Mother Teresa?" excerpted from *A Retreat With Mother Teresa and Damien of Molokai: Caring for Those Who Suffer,* by Joan Guntzelman, www.americancatholic.org (5/30/2012).

[2] From *Nobel Lectures, Peace 1971-1980,* Ed. Ed.-in-Charge Tore Frängsmyr, Ed. Irwin Abrams (Singapore: World Scientific Publishing Co., 1997), www,nobelprize.org (6/13/12).

[3] "Mother Teresa of Calcutta (1970-1977)," www.vatican.va/The Holy See/English/search/Mother Teresa of Calcutta (1910-1977), biography.

Missionaries of Charity:

As soon as Teresa got well, she returned to launch the Missionaries of Charity. To be a well-trained servant, she first completed a course in medical missions, so she could take care of the sick and dying.

But starting her ministry was no cakewalk. She spent her time in the slums (the poorest parts of town). Leprosy was an especially common disease in the area. Anyone here know what leprosy is? *(Get answer from Superkids.)*

Leprosy is a disease that eats away at people's flesh[4]. A lot of people with leprosy may have missing fingers, toes, noses and ears. So, as you can imagine, people with leprosy were difficult to look at, and most people avoided them. But this didn't stop Teresa. She knew God had called her to serve the unwanted and hurting. The little kids in the area loved her sweet spirit and began calling her "Mother."

At first, her ministry only had two people. It would take money to start a mission. Mother Teresa spent all she had on others, so she had to beg for food. She even sold a beautiful car that was given to her to set up a place to help people with leprosy in India. She knew being a servant was way bigger and better than having lots of money.

Besides, with a God who promises that servants will be the GREATEST of all—how could she worry about money? Surely, He would take care of things! After a tough year, her big servant's heart didn't just have God's attention, it also got the attention of the government of India and her church. That's when things really exploded for Mother Teresa.

Pure Heart:

The Indian government appreciated how Mother Teresa was taking care of their unwanted, unloved people, so they gave her an abandoned building next to a Hindu temple to use as her first mission house, which she named, in the Indian language, *Nirmal Hriday* or "Pure Heart." And that's certainly what Mother Teresa had—a pure heart! Over time, God made sure Mother Teresa had all the tools she needed to show His love to people on every continent.

Making History:

All over the world, people still know Mother Teresa as one of the greatest servants of all time. By the time she died in 1997, she had over 4,000 missionaries working with her, and 610 mission houses in 123 countries[5]! She also won several famous awards for her amazing servant's heart, like the Nobel Peace Prize in 1979. But none of this mattered much to Mother Teresa. She just replied, "I am a little pencil in the hand of a writing God who is sending a love letter to the world."

Outro:

One of the quickest ways to spot a true servant is to look for someone who serves others because they love, not because they want to be honored or given awards. Mother Teresa's hope was that people would think less of her and more of Jesus. And she definitely accomplished that when she reached out to serve the hurting, unwanted and unloved. That is exactly why Mother Teresa is the subject of today's Real Deal.

---

[4] World Health Organization: "Leprosy," www.who.int/mediacentre/factsheets/fs101/en/index.html.

[5] "Mother Teresa of Calcutta (1910-1997)," search www.vatican.va (5/30/2012).

Notes: _____

_____

_____

_____

_____

_____

_____

_____

_____

_____

_____

_____

_____

_____

_____

_____

_____

_____

_____

_____

_____

_____

_____

_____

_____

_____

_____

_____

_____

_____

_____

_____

_____

_____

DAY 5: GAME TIME — FUN CEREAL FEED

Suggested Time: 5-10 minutes

Memory Verse: Honor your father and mother. Love your neighbor as yourself.—Matthew 19:19

Supplies: ☐ 2-4 Plastic spoons, ☐ 2-4 Small, plastic-handled goldfish-type nets, ☐ 2 Bowls, ☐ 1 Box of breakfast cereal, ☐ 2 Chairs, ☐ Small prop table (to place game items), ☐ Upbeat game music to play during game

Prior to Game:

Set up table. Place all game items on table. Pour cereal into each bowl. Set chairs up so that they are back to back with seats visible to the audience.

Game Instructions:

Today, we're learning about serving our neighbor. You may think that sounds like no fun, but wait until you see how we're going to practice! We're going to practice serving our neighbor some yummy breakfast cereal.

Does anyone want to serve his or her neighbor?

Divide players into two teams of two. Have one player per team kneel on a chair, while holding a bowl of dry breakfast cereal. If two teams are not an option, have players switch places and see who can collect more cereal in their net at the end.

One player per team will have a plastic spoon handle in his or her mouth. The other player will sit cross-legged on the floor in front of the chair, with a net handle held in between his or her front teeth. Have that player place hands in his or her lap or behind the back.

At the start of game music, the players with the cereal will scoop it with their spoons and fill the net as full as possible before the music stops. No hands! The kids may, of course, eat the cereal in their bowls and nets at the end!

Game Goal:

Practice serving your neighbor. It can be so much fun!

Final Word:

A lot of people think serving others is no fun, but we just proved it's a blast, especially when it means serving up some yummy cereal!

Variation: Fish-Feeding Frenzy:

If your kids don't enjoy cereal or you prefer something less sweet for a snack, try small, cheesy, fish-shaped crackers. They'd be fun to scoop into the fish nets.

ACTIVITY PAGE — GOOD NEIGHBOR CROSSWORD

Memory Verse: Honor your father and mother. Love your neighbor as yourself.—Matthew 19:19

You've been learning what it means to be a good neighbor. In your Bible lesson this week, you read the story of the Good Samaritan as told by Jesus. It's a powerful story of how important it is to reach out to people in need. See how well you learned that story by using words from it to complete this crossword puzzle.

Across
3. a Jewish synagogue
6. a very short story told to teach a moral or lesson
8. a feeling of sharing another's suffering that leads to a desire to help
10. a native or citizen of Samaria

Down
1. a mammal with hooves that is closely related to the horse
2. the capital city of Israel
4. a person who is authorized by a church to lead prayers and religious services
5. kind treatment by someone who has some power over another
7. a small hotel for people who are traveling
9. a robber who is often a member of a gang that robs people while they are traveling

ANSWER KEY

Across
3. temple
6. parable
8. compassion
10. Samaritan

Down
1. donkey
2. Jerusalem
4. priest
5. mercy
7. inn
8. bandit

Notes: _____

_____

_____

_____

_____

_____

_____

_____

_____

_____

_____

_____

_____

_____

_____

_____

_____

_____

_____

_____

_____

_____

WEEK 10: SERVING STARTS AT HOME

Memory Verse: For even the Son of Man came not to be served but to serve others and to give his life as a ransom for many.—Matthew 20:28

WEEK 10: SNAPSHOT

SERVING STARTS AT HOME

DAY	TYPE OF LESSON	LESSON TITLE	SUPPLIES
Day 1	Bible Lesson	David Serves	None
Day 2	Read-Aloud	The Witness Zone: "Clean House, Win Big"	None
Day 3	Giving Lesson	A Labor of Love	Homemade cookies, Glass of milk, Sleeping bag, Party hat, Kid's sport uniform
Day 4	Food Fun	Oatmeal Anyone?	Griddle, Pancake turner, 1 Small and 1 large mixing bowl, Large spoon, Plates and forks, 6 Strips of bacon, 1-1/2 Cups quick-cooking oatmeal, 2 Cups milk, 1 Cup flour, 2 Tablespoons packed brown sugar, 2 Teaspoons baking powder, 1 Teaspoon salt, 3 Eggs, 1/4 Cup butter, Butter and maple syrup to top pancakes
Day 5	Game Time	You Got Served	2 Regular metal spoons, Bag of small marshmallows, 2 Plastic cups, Table
Bonus	Activity Page	King David's Color-by-Number	1 Copy for each child

Lesson Introduction:

This is one of my favorite lessons to teach children. If we can explain what a great (and rewarding) thing it is to serve, we can lay a foundation that will stand throughout our children's entire lives. This is where the rubber meets the road. One thing I like to do is describe the benefits of serving someone and then enjoying watching them be blessed. Christmas morning can be a great example of how much fun it is to watch someone open a gift we have prepared for them. It is truly more blessed to give than to receive!

Avoid talking about serving like you would a chore that needs to be done. Jesus did not serve us, waiting for the day it would finally be over. Instead, "He ever lives to make intercession for us" (Hebrews 7:5)! I suggest giving your children a "serving challenge" for the upcoming week. Next week, have two or three of them who have a good report to share, tell what it was like to observe the fruit of serving. Being a servant should become one of the most fun things any of us do. The perspective of Jesus is the best one we can have!

Commander Dana
Commander Dana

Lesson Outline:

This week, as you focus on serving, remind your kids that the rewards of serving are amazing, even though that's not the reason we serve! We do it because we love Jesus who loved us enough to humbly serve and give His life. Now *that's* servanthood!

I. JESUS WAS THE ULTIMATE SERVANT Philippians 2:7

a. He served His father by working with him. Matthew 13:55

b. He served His parents even when He was busy for God! Luke 2:42-51

c. Even as a grown-up, Jesus knew how to serve His family. John 2:3-8

II. START SMALL, GROW GREAT! Matthew 20:26

a. A boy named David knew about serving. 1 Samuel 16:11

b. He also served as a musician and messenger. 1 Samuel 16:18-19, 17:18-19

c. "David the servant" became "David the king"—Israel's most famous!

III. SERVING HAS GREATER REWARDS THAN BEING SERVED Mark 9:35

a. Some people prefer to be waited on by others.

b. In God's kingdom, it works the opposite way! Galatians 6:7

c. Loving and serving our family prepares us to serve and love God. 1 John 4:20

Notes:_____

_____

_____

_____

_____

_____

_____

DAY 1: BIBLE LESSON — DAVID SERVES

Memory Verse: *For even the Son of Man came not to be served but to serve others and to give his life as a ransom for many.*—Matthew 20:28

This week, your family will focus on the life of David, before he was king of Israel. You'll note he serves as a shepherd, a musician and food server to his brothers. You'll find one thing evident in God's Word about David from the beginning—his *heart* was different! Be keenly aware of the gifts God has placed within your children and encourage those who have a servant's heart. God will use them mightily to accomplish His purposes!

Read 1 Samuel 16:11-19; 17:18-19:
David Serves His Father

Then Samuel asked, "Are these all the sons you have?"

"There is still the youngest," Jesse replied. "But he's out in the fields watching the sheep and goats."

"Send for him at once," Samuel said. "We will not sit down to eat until he arrives."

So Jesse sent for him. He was dark and handsome, with beautiful eyes.

And the Lord said, "This is the one; anoint him."

So as David stood there among his brothers, Samuel took the flask of olive oil he had brought and anointed David with the oil. And the Spirit of the Lord came powerfully upon David from that day on. Then Samuel returned to Ramah.

David Serves in Saul's Court

Now the Spirit of the Lord had left Saul...Some of Saul's servants said to him,... "Let us find a good musician to play the harp whenever the tormenting spirit troubles you. He will play soothing music, and you will soon be well again."

"All right," Saul said. "Find me someone who plays well, and bring him here."

One of the servants said to Saul, "One of Jesse's sons from Bethlehem is a talented harp player. Not only that—he is a brave warrior, a man of war, and has good judgment. He is also a fine-looking young man, and the Lord is with him."

David Serves His Brothers

"And give these ten cuts of cheese to their captain. See how your brothers are getting along, and bring back a report on how they are doing." David's brothers were with Saul and the Israelite army at the valley of Elah, fighting against the Philistines.

Discussion Questions:

1. **How was David chosen to be king of Israel?**
   God sent the prophet Samuel to anoint him and told Samuel that David was to be the next king.

2. **What job had David been doing when Samuel came to anoint him to be king?**
   He was the family's shepherd.

3. **What was David's job in serving King Saul?**
   He was a musician and played the harp to calm the king.

4. **How did David serve his brothers?**
   He took cheese and bread to them from his father when his brothers were in the army.

5. **Why is it important to look at David's early life?**
   Answers will vary. He became king and was noted as a "man after my [God's] own heart" (1 Samuel 13:14; Acts 13:22). He practiced serving others before others served him.

6. **What can I learn from this passage?**
   Answers will vary, but they should point to how your children can serve God and others. Practical application answers are especially good.

Notes: _____

_____

_____

_____

_____

_____

_____

_____

_____

_____

_____

_____

_____

_____

_____

_____

_____

_____

_____

_____

DAY 2: READ-ALOUD

THE WITNESS ZONE: "CLEAN HOUSE, WIN BIG"

Suggested Time: 15 minutes

Memory Verse: For even the Son of Man came not to be served but to serve others and to give his life as a ransom for many.—Matthew 20:28

Lesson Instructions:

You are about to enter a zone unlike any other, where normal life becomes anything but normal and everyday conversations go from ordinary to shocking in the blink of an eye. It's a place where eternal choices are made—where faith meets fear, and boldness meets hesitation. It's a zone where kids can become history makers or bolt like a runaway train. Buckle your seat belts and hold on for the ride. You are about to enter…"The Witness Zone!"

There's Skyler, sitting at a table with a fruit bowl in the middle of it, eating a toaster pastry and reading the box, when his mom enters and sits down with a coffee cup in her hand.

"Good morning, Skyler," his mom says. "I thought I told you to eat something healthy for breakfast."

"I am. Look." Skyler holds up the box. "These toaster pastries are made with real fruit flavors. See?"

"Real Fruit FLAVORS, huh?" his mom says. "Well, before you finish your fruit FLAVORS, I want you to have a real piece of fruit."

Skyler says, "OK."

"And, I want you to go make your bed," his mom adds.

"But, you're the mom—aren't *you* supposed to do that? Tim's mom still makes his bed. And, she cleans his room," Skyler says.

"Well, I'm not Tim's mom, and you're not Tim. I'm *your* mom. And if you want to keep arguing about it, you can make my bed, too."

"Man! I hate making the bed," Skyler whines. "It's my least favorite chore."

"You said taking out the trash was your least favorite chore," his mom says.

"That too," Skyler admits, finishing his toaster pastry.

"And, setting the table, and doing the dishes…"

"Yeah. Chores stink," Skyler says.

"Well, stink or not, that's life," his mom says. "I can't work, make meals and clean the house all by myself. So, go make your bed."

"All right, all right. I'm going." Skyler shuffles slowly out of the room.

(Discuss what your children think about how Skyler acted. Was Skyler a good witness to his mother? Why or why not?)

What you just witnessed was a lazy young person who doesn't realize how much he could impact his unsaved mom by being a servant. When Skyler whines about helping out around the house, "The Witness Zone" door slams shut. Let's see what happens when he has a servant's heart instead.

Alternate Ending:

There's Skyler, sitting at a table with a fruit bowl in the middle of it, eating a toaster pastry and reading the box, when his mom enters and sits down with a coffee cup in her hand.

"Good morning, Skyler," his mom says. "I thought I told you to eat something healthy for breakfast."

"I am. Look." Skyler holds up the box. "These toaster pastries are made with real fruit flavors. See?"

"Real Fruit FLAVORS, huh?" his mom says. "Well, before you finish your fruit FLAVORS, I want you to have a real piece of fruit."

"Yes, ma'am," Skyler says cheerfully.

"Skyler, I need to ask you about something," his mom asks slowly. "Why have you been cleaning my room? And, I noticed you cleaned the bathrooms and the kitchen floor."

"Well, it's part of my 'Start Small, Grow Great' plan," Skyler explains.

"Which is what?" his mom asks curiously.

"I learned it at Superkid Academy," Skyler says. "The Bible says that if you want to be great, then start small. That just means serve other people, instead of wanting to be served. And, the best place to start is with your family!"

"Huh. That's interesting," his mom says. "The Bible really says that?"

"Yes, ma'am." Skyler smiles and takes his last bite of toaster pastry.

There you have it, another open door, another victory. A challenge given and a challenge met. When Skyler goes the extra mile to help his mom around the house, instead of complaining, his mom can't help but be impressed. Skyler's heart to serve opens the door to talk to his mom about Jesus, and two weeks later he leads her in a salvation prayer. Whoever would have thought that cleaning house would win his mom to Jesus?

Discussion Questions:

Use these questions as conversation starters. Let this be a personal time of sharing with your children:

1. How can we witness through our actions?

2. What do you think of the saying, "Actions speak louder than words"? How does that apply in this story? How does it apply in our lives?

3. If there are unsaved members in your family, discuss how your family could witness to them through serving.

Notes: _____

_____

_____

_____

_____

_____

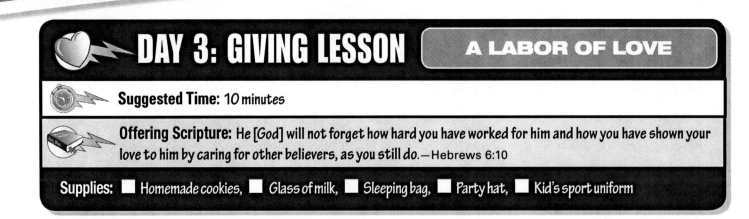

DAY 3: GIVING LESSON — A LABOR OF LOVE

Suggested Time: 10 minutes

Offering Scripture: He [God] will not forget how hard you have worked for him and how you have shown your love to him by caring for other believers, as you still do. —Hebrews 6:10

Supplies: ☐ Homemade cookies, ☐ Glass of milk, ☐ Sleeping bag, ☐ Party hat, ☐ Kid's sport uniform

Lesson Instructions:

I have some items today that remind me of different events and thought you might like to guess what each thing reminds me of. Do you think you can guess what my clues mean?

OK, the first clue actually has two parts: a sleeping bag and a party hat. Who can guess what I'm thinking of? *(Get some answers from your kids.)*

Of course: a sleepover party!

Let's move on to clue No. 2: a baseball uniform *(or whatever uniform you have available).* What does this make you think of?

Yes, a baseball game.

For my last clue—this one is a little tougher than the others. I have here some homemade cookies and a glass of milk. What could this possibly make you think of? *(Take some guesses; you may not get a correct answer on this one.)*

The cookies and milk make me think of an afternoon snack.

Kids, all of these things—a sleepover party, a baseball game and afternoon snacks—have something in common. All of them involved someone working hard to do something nice for a person they love. If you've ever had a sleepover, your dad and I had a lot to do to get ready. We got together lots of snacks for your guests, rented a movie or planned some games, and then we had to get up and make breakfast after not sleeping all night!

When you were part of a sports team, someone had to wash your uniform, take you to practices and then show up to watch your games. And, maybe you have walked into the house after playing outside and I had some delicious, warm cookies or other treat for you with a nice, cold glass of milk. Do you know why moms and dads do all these things? It's because they love their kids!

In Hebrews 6:10, God's Word talks about people who work hard because they love others. The scripture says, "He [God] will not forget how hard you have worked for him and how you have shown your love to him by caring for other believers, as you still do." It is so awesome to realize that when we do things that will bless others just because we love them, God notices and promises not to forget our hard work.

Why don't we let our awesome God know that, just like He remembers what good things we do, we remember all the amazing things He has done for us by preparing Him an offering today?

Variation No. 1: Personal Mementos

Feel free to personalize the objects in this lesson to reflect your family. If your child takes dance or gymnastics class, for example, then use the appropriate apparel. If your child takes martial arts, then include those items. The "items" could even be your child's pet or their clothes, which you buy and wash.

Variation No. 2: Friend Party

Let your kids plan a "Just Because" party, and invite their friends. Let them do all the work: planning, preparing, even shopping. Walk them through each step of the preparations you would normally do by yourself. Then remind them why you do it for them! It's because you love them. God also does so many amazing things for us—just because He loves us!

Notes: _____

_____

_____

_____

_____

_____

_____

_____

_____

_____

_____

_____

_____

_____

_____

_____

_____

_____

_____

_____

_____

_____

_____

_____

_____

_____

_____

DAY 4: FOOD FUN

OATMEAL ANYONE?

Suggested Time: 10 minutes

Memory Verse: For even the Son of Man came not to be served but to serve others and to give his life as a ransom for many.—Matthew 20:28

Bacon-Oatmeal Pancake Recipe:

Ingredients: ☐ 6 Strips of bacon, cooked crisp and crumbled, ☐ 1 1/2 Cups quick-cooking oatmeal ☐ 2 Cups milk ☐ 1 Cup flour, ☐ 2 Tablespoons packed brown sugar, ☐ 2 Teaspoons baking powder, ☐ 1 Teaspoon salt, ☐ 3 Eggs, beaten, ☐ 1/4 Cup melted butter, cooled, ☐ Butter and maple syrup to top pancakes

1. Mix oatmeal and milk in large bowl and set aside until all milk has been absorbed.

2. Combine flour, brown sugar, baking powder and salt in small bowl.

3. Add eggs and bacon to the oatmeal mixture; mix well.

4. Stir in flour mixture; add butter and stir only long enough to blend batter. Do not overmix!

5. Lightly butter griddle and heat to medium-high, until water drop flicked onto pan "dances" around.

6. Pour batter in pan; cook 2-3 minutes until small bubbles form around edges and start to break.

7. Flip pancakes over and brown other side.

8. Butter and top with warm syrup. Mmmmm!

Supplies: ☐ Griddle, ☐ Pancake turner, ☐ 1 Small and 1 large mixing bowl, ☐ Large spoon (for mixing) ☐ Plates and forks

Lesson Instructions:

What have we been learning the last few weeks? We've learned what God's Word says about being a servant. First, we found out that if you want to be great in God's eyes, you must have a heart to serve other people. Last week we learned that the Bible tells us to love our neighbor. That just means to reach out and help anyone we see who is hurt, in trouble or just plain lonely.

But today, we are talking about one of the most important things to know about being a servant. We may know that it's important to serve others, but don't you think it would be a good idea to find out where the best place to start is?

Guess what? The best place to begin is right in our own house! I think God wants us to start here first because sometimes that's the hardest place to be a servant. And, if we learn how to serve our moms and dads and brothers and sisters, then it will be pretty simple for us to serve and bless the other people the Lord brings into our lives.

Now that we know where to start, I think it would be fun to work on an idea of how to get started! Today, we are going to learn how to make something delicious for our family.

Shall we get started? I have a great new recipe to try. *(Proceed to cook the pancakes.)*

Wow, I had a great time cooking with you all this morning! Did you have any idea that being a servant could be such fun?

Notes: _____

_____

_____

_____

_____

_____

_____

_____

_____

_____

_____

_____

_____

_____

_____

_____

_____

_____

_____

_____

_____

_____

_____

_____

_____

_____

_____

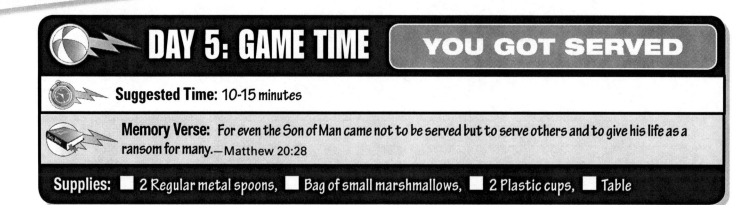

DAY 5: GAME TIME — YOU GOT SERVED

Suggested Time: 10-15 minutes

Memory Verse: For even the Son of Man came not to be served but to serve others and to give his life as a ransom for many.—Matthew 20:28

Supplies: ☐ 2 Regular metal spoons, ☐ Bag of small marshmallows, ☐ 2 Plastic cups, ☐ Table

Prior to Game:

Divide the marshmallows into two piles at opposite ends of table, with a spoon and a cup by each pile.

Game Instructions:

- Review the memory verse with your kids. This game requires a team of two working together. If you have more than one team, have players switch positions and then count which one caught more in their cup.
- One person "serves" the marshmallows, the other one tries to catch them in his/her cup.
- At the signal to start, "servers" place a single marshmallow on the handle end of their spoon, which lays flat on the end of the table.
- Prior to each "serve," players must say the memory verse out loud!
- The server pushes down on the spoon, which launches the marshmallow into the air. The catcher tries to catch it in the cup.

Variation No. 1: Small Group

Write the verse on a whiteboard, or for a smaller group, use a stopwatch to time how long it takes for the kids to catch a certain number of marshmallows in their cups.

Variation No. 2: Party Time

Invite friends over to expand the size of your group and share your memory verse as well.

Game Goal:

The player with the most catches wins this wacky game!

Final Word:

Review the memory verse that you've hidden in your hearts. What a great way to hide God's Word in your heart! While you're having fun and being silly, you can take a moment to remember that God's Word is powerful and alive within you!

ACTIVITY PAGE — KING DAVID'S COLOR-BY-NUMBER

Memory Verse: For even the Son of Man came not to be served but to serve others and to give his life as a ransom for many.—Matthew 20:28

We can learn a lot about how to serve God and others by studying King David. In Acts 13:22, the Bible refers to him as a "man after my [God's] own heart." In addition, King David was a man of many talents. Complete this color-by-number to find out something King David used in one of his jobs before he was king.

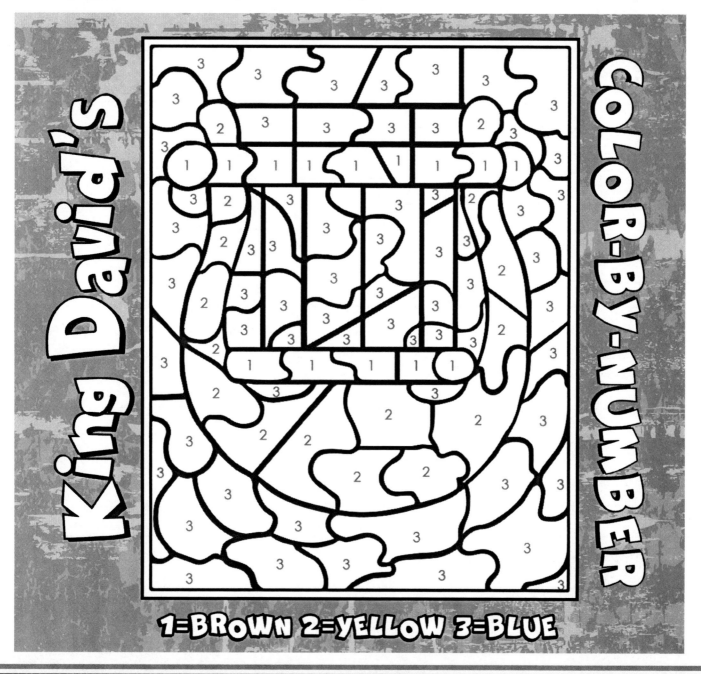

King David's COLOR-BY-NUMBER

1=BROWN 2=YELLOW 3=BLUE

Notes: _____

_____

_____

_____

_____

_____

_____

_____

_____

_____

_____

_____

_____

_____

_____

_____

_____

_____

_____

_____

_____

_____

_____

_____

_____

_____

_____

_____

_____

_____

_____

_____

_____

_____

WEEK 11: GOD SAYS YOU ARE CHOSEN

Memory Verse: For God knew his people in advance, and he chose them to become like his Son, so that his Son would be the firstborn among many brothers and sisters. —Romans 8:29

WEEK 11: SNAPSHOT

GOD SAYS YOU ARE CHOSEN

DAY	TYPE OF LESSON	LESSON TITLE	SUPPLIES
Day 1	Bible Lesson	Following Jesus	None
Day 2	Academy Lab	Dive In	Cutting board (plastic is best), Clear glass of water, Small matchbox, Raw egg
Day 3	Giving Lesson	Answer That Call!	Cell phone, Prearranged text/call or ring tone alarm
Day 4	Real Deal	Galileo Galilei	**Optional costume/prop:** Gray beard, Black robe, Telescope
Day 5	Game Time	You Choose!	Large bag or box, Blindfold, 12-20 Miscellaneous items, Table, Timer
Bonus	Activity Page	Scripture Memory Match	1 Copy for each child

Lesson Introduction:

It is important for us to realize the great call on this generation today! God is calling them to come to a place of total dedication to Him. In John 6:44-45 Jesus repeats for the second time that He will raise up a Body of believers at the last day, then He says those believers will all be taught by God, quoting Isaiah 54. This refers to children. As you teach your children this week, keep that in mind. Jesus spoke of children in the last days rising up to believe in Him and do miracles! I believe He spoke of *our* children! Will they choose to be chosen?

Lead your kids to make some important decisions today.

- Do they want to be God's people, His kids?

- Will they exchange His thoughts for their thoughts?

- Will they be like the disciples and drop everything? Or will they be like the young man who let his possessions keep him from following Jesus?

- Will they join Jesus' team and win people to Him, wearing His royal clothing of love and kindness (the fruit of the spirit)?

I know they will as God makes His appeal through you. You are anointed for such a time as this!

Love,

Commander Kellie

Commander Kellie

Lesson Outline:

This week you'll be studying about destiny and God's purpose in choosing *you* and *your children* for this time to accomplish His purposes. He knows you and your family and has a divine plan for each member! How breathtakingly awesome!

I.   HE KNEW US BEFORE WE KNEW HIM

a. He loved us and chose us before He made the world. Ephesians 1:4

b. He chose us to be His own people. 1 Thessalonians 1:4

c. He chose us to be His family. Romans 8:29

II. HE'S CHOSEN US TO BE LIKE JESUS, OUR BROTHER Romans 8:29

a. Jesus chose disciples to follow Him. "Come follow Me," He said. They dropped everything to follow Jesus.

b. Although Jesus chose him, the rich young ruler let his love for things keep him from following. Mark 10:17-22

c. He has chosen us to follow Him, look like Him and love like Him. Will you follow? John 15:14-17

III. MANY ARE CALLED, FEW ARE CHOSEN Matthew 22:14

a. You have to show up to be chosen. Matthew 22:1-10

b. Be dressed and ready. Matthew 22:11-14; Colossians 3:12-14

c. We must choose to be chosen! 1 Peter 2:6-9

Notes: _____

_____

_____

_____

_____

_____

_____

_____

_____

_____

DAY 1: BIBLE LESSON — FOLLOWING JESUS

Memory Verse: *For God knew his people in advance, and he chose them to become like his Son, so that his Son would be the firstborn among many brothers and sisters.*—Romans 8:29

Sometimes it's easy to think of the disciples as people who just followed Jesus around without minds and thoughts of their own…just the workers who Jesus used to feed a crowd or help Him slip away when He was exhausted. But it wasn't easy for the disciples to drop everything they owned, to leave their families and their occupations, and to follow Him. For everyone who follows Jesus, there is a moment of decision that is uniquely personal. Make sure your kids realize they have the *choice* to follow Christ. Christ came to show us a better way to live, but the first step is in the choosing. Pray that your kids choose to follow Him today!

Read Mark 10:17-31:
The Rich Man

As Jesus was starting out on his way to Jerusalem, a man came running up to him, knelt down, and asked, "Good Teacher, what must I do to inherit eternal life?"

"Why do you call me good?" Jesus asked. "Only God is truly good. But to answer your question, you know the commandments: 'You must not murder. You must not commit adultery. You must not steal. You must not testify falsely. You must not cheat anyone. Honor your father and mother.'"

"Teacher," the man replied, "I've obeyed all these commandments since I was young."

Looking at the man, Jesus felt genuine love for him. "There is still one thing you haven't done," he told him. "Go and sell all your possessions and give the money to the poor, and you will have treasure in heaven. Then come, follow me."

At this the man's face fell, and he went away sad, for he had many possessions.

Jesus looked around and said to his disciples, "How hard it is for the rich to enter the Kingdom of God!" This amazed them. But Jesus said again, "Dear children, it is very hard to enter the Kingdom of God. In fact, it is easier for a camel to go through the eye of a needle than for a rich person to enter the Kingdom of God!"

The disciples were astounded. "Then who in the world can be saved?" they asked.

Jesus looked at them intently and said, "Humanly speaking, it is impossible. But not with God. Everything is possible with God."

Then Peter began to speak up. "We've given up everything to follow you," he said.

"Yes," Jesus replied, "and I assure you that everyone who has given up house or brothers or sisters or mother or father or children or property, for my sake and for the Good News, will receive now in return a hundred times as many houses, brothers, sisters, mothers, children, and property—along with persecution. And in the world to come that person will have eternal life. But many who are the greatest now will be least important then, and those who seem least important now will be the greatest then."

Discussion Questions:

1. **Tell me three things that happened in this passage.**
   Answers will vary. Make sure they include Jesus, the disciples and the rich man.

2. **What did Jesus tell the man to do that was difficult?**
   Jesus told him to sell all his possessions and give them to the poor.

3. **Why was this so difficult for him?**
   This man was rich and had many things. He loved those things more than he wanted to follow Jesus.

4. **What else did Jesus ask him?**
   Jesus asked if he had kept the Ten Commandments.

5. **What was his response?**
   He said he had kept all of them since he was young.

6. **Why was it significant that Jesus asked him to give away all his riches and follow Him?**
   Jesus was asking the man to not only obey the law, but to actually walk with Him and fellowship with Him. That was the part the man was not willing to do. Because of that choice, he did not choose eternal life.

7. **What was Peter's response?**
   We've given up everything to follow You, Jesus.

8. **Why does Jesus ask us to give up "stuff" to follow Him?**
   He knows there are things that will distract us from His purpose and keep us from following Him. He wants us to treasure Him above all else.

9. **Have you made the decision to follow Jesus?**
   Listen attentively and allow the Holy Spirit to guide you with your children if any of them have not chosen to follow Jesus yet.

Notes: _____

_____

_____

_____

_____

_____

_____

_____

_____

_____

_____

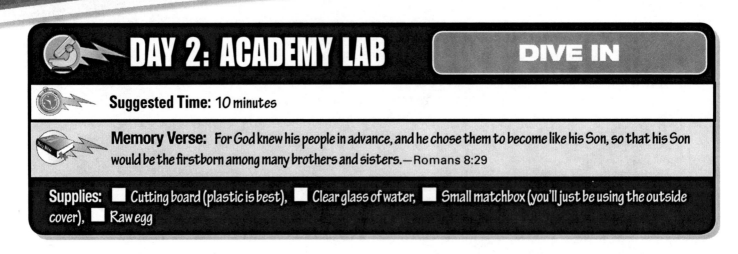

DAY 2: ACADEMY LAB

DIVE IN

Suggested Time: *10 minutes*

Memory Verse: *For God knew his people in advance, and he chose them to become like his Son, so that his Son would be the firstborn among many brothers and sisters.*—Romans 8:29

Supplies: ☐ Cutting board (plastic is best), ☐ Clear glass of water, ☐ Small matchbox (you'll just be using the outside cover), ☐ Raw egg

Experiment:

1. Place the cutting board on top of the glass of water.

2. Now place the matchbox cover (without the inside part) on the cutting board, centered over the glass of water.

3. Gently balance the egg on top of the matchbox case.

4. Next is the fun part: You are going to transfer the egg into the water without breaking it. To do this, pull the board sharply to one side and the egg should fall into the glass.

5. If done right, the egg should fall into the water, and the matchbox will fly off to the side. To have a little more fun with this, your assistant can challenge whether the egg was indeed raw, at which point you can break it into his/her hand.

Lesson Instructions:

Today, we are learning what it means to be chosen by God. Each of us has probably had some experience with being chosen for a team or special performance of some kind. Being chosen by God to do something special for Him is a big step up from playing baseball or dancing in a recital, wouldn't you agree?

We're going to do a fun, little experiment that reminds me of one of the requirements for being chosen by God. The first thing we will be using is this ordinary glass of water. Let's just set it right in the middle of the table. We will call this glass of water "God's plan for me."

Next, we will place a cutting board on top of the glass. The cutting board will be called "I'm just a kid." Sometimes, when you think things like, "I'm too young to do anything for God," it can be the very thing standing between you and "God's plan for me."

Now, for the third step. I'm going to set a matchbox case in the center of our "I'm just a kid" cutting board and we'll name it "But what can I do?" If we get stuck on being concerned about our own abilities—what we can and can't do—we will never have the courage to step out and follow God's plan for us.

OK, now the tricky part. I have a raw egg.

What should we call this egg? *(Accept fun responses.)*

This egg is YOU! I'm now going to take you and balance you right on top of "God's plan for me," "I'm just a kid," and "But what can I do?" In Romans 8:29 it says, "For God knew his people in advance, and he chose them to become like his Son, so that his Son would be the firstborn among many brothers and sisters." But did you realize that, even though God chose you to be like Jesus, there is a part that you have to do? Let me show you what that part is. *(Complete the experiment by following the remaining steps.)* Did you see how, when the "I'm just a kid" cutting board and "But what can I do?" matchbox were moved out of the way, the egg fell right into the "God's plan for me" glass of water?

Well, that's just like what happens with us when we move thoughts like, "I'm just a kid" or "But what can I do?" out of the way and dive straight into "God's plan for me." And, guess what? There's a little bonus, too. When we decide to dive into God's plan, it's a nice, safe place to land!

Notes: _____

_____

_____

_____

_____

_____

_____

_____

_____

_____

_____

_____

_____

_____

_____

_____

_____

_____

_____

_____

_____

_____

_____

_____

_____

_____

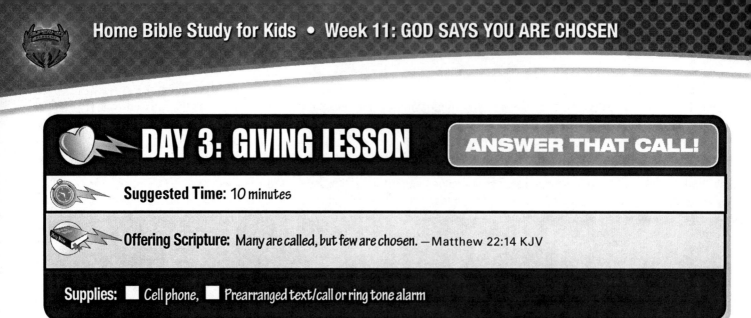

DAY 3: GIVING LESSON

ANSWER THAT CALL!

Suggested Time: *10 minutes*

Offering Scripture: *Many are called, but few are chosen.* —Matthew 22:14 KJV

Supplies: ■ Cell phone, ■ Prearranged text/call or ring tone alarm

Lesson Instructions:

Today, we are going to look at a very important truth in God's Word. Let's read it from Matthew 22:14. It says, "Many are called, but few are chosen." What's cool about this verse is that God calls many. I like that!

Would you like for God to call you? *(Allow your Superkids to respond, and at this time your phone should ring or receive a text.)*

Excuse me, this looks important *(answer phone)*. "This is _____, may I help you? Oh, hello!"

(Pause while listening to phone.) "Really? That's too bad. Well, you can count on me, I'll be there."

(short pause) "What's that?"

(pause) "Wow, that sounds awesome! See you tomorrow!"

(Turn to your kids and let them in on your phone call.)

The most interesting thing has happened. My friend called a lot of (his/her)friends to invite them to dinner, but none of them could go. I said yes when they called, and guess what? It's not an ordinary dinner. A limo is picking us up and taking us to dinner at an amazing restaurant. We are having a dessert sampler with seven desserts! Then, we are going to a movie with free all-you-can-eat concessions. The best part is it's all paid for! I'm so glad I answered that call!

(Hold up your phone and explain to your kids.)

Now that you've seen me act out a little drama, I want you to understand what Matthew 22:14 is really talking about. If we don't answer when God calls, He cannot choose us for the great things He has planned. Did you know that God calls us to be givers, and He would like to prosper us big-time? It's true! Too many times, believers like you and me will get that call from God, and we won't answer. We think, *Someone else can give to the poor. They don't really need me. I can't do very much.*

The truth is, when we answer the call that is in God's Word and do what He tells us, we are on His list of those He can choose for the really special things. I want to be chosen, but first I have to do the right thing when God calls me. Many get the call to be givers—will you be on the chosen list? Let's prepare our offering now and answer God's call to help others through our church!

Notes: _____

_____

_____

DAY 4: REAL DEAL — GALILEO GALILEI

Memory Verse: For God knew his people in advance, and he chose them to become like his Son, so that his Son would be the firstborn among many brothers and sisters.—Romans 8:29

Concept: Highlighting an interesting historical place, figure or event that illustrates the theme of the day. The theme of the day is God says you are chosen.

Media: If you have the technical capability, show DVDs that feature photos of Galileo. If you do not have this capability, you may print out photos from the Internet to show the kids.

Teacher Tip: Entering in costume is an attention grabber for your children. When presenting the information, it's helpful to have pictures and books available, too.

Optional Costume/Prop: ☐ Gray beard, ☐ Black robe, ☐ Telescope

Intro:

Today, we're talking about being chosen by God. When God chooses someone, He always chooses them to do and be something great. All you have to do is read your Bible to know that's true. Abraham, Moses, Joseph, Paul, Peter…they were all chosen by God to change their world. And because they stayed ready, they did!

But they weren't the only ones to stay ready to change their world. One Italian man, born the same year as William Shakespeare, was ready to answer God's call, too. He changed the way people would think about the universe forever! This mystery man is called the "Father of Modern Science" and was the first person ever to look at the universe using a telescope. Any guesses who he was?

Lesson Instructions:
About Galileo Galilei:

This mystery man's name was Galileo Galilei. Galileo was born in 1564, and was the oldest of four kids. Until age 10, he was taught by his father, Vincenzio—a talented musician and mathematician. But, when his family moved to Florence, Italy, the next year, Galileo went to school.

The Call:

As a young person, Galileo thought about going into church ministry, but his father urged him to follow his gifts, and he ended up going to college to study mathematics instead. By age 25, Galileo had become so good at mathematics that he was appointed leader of math at the university.

During this time, he made some big discoveries in science.

The First Step—A Telescope:

In 1608, Hans Lippershey of the Netherlands[6] invented the first simple telescope, but it wasn't very strong. Galileo set out to make it strong enough to view outer space. By the next year, he had done it! He was able to develop a telescope 30 times stronger than the original invention. Galileo was then able to sell his new and improved telescopes to the government and to sea-ship captains to make some extra money. And, extra money was what it would take for Galileo to keep up his scientific work.

The Second Step—Jupiter's Moons:

Just five months later, Galileo made an amazing discovery while looking at Jupiter through his telescope. He noticed there were four moons turning around the planet[7]. No one had ever seen these moons before. He named them after one of his heroes, Medici, but later astronomers renamed them the "Galilean satellites" in Galileo's honor.

The Big Discovery:

Spotting moons spinning around Jupiter was important for one humongous reason: This helped Galileo prove something most of the world didn't believe. At that time, nearly all scientists and astronomers believed that the sun circled the earth. But Galileo agreed with another famous astronomer named Copernicus, that the earth circled the sun, instead.

Because the moons spun around Jupiter while Jupiter spun around the sun, it proved that one planet can spin around another, while that planet spins around a different planet. Sound confusing? It's enough to make your head spin…but it made perfect sense to Galileo. No wonder he was chosen to make this great discovery! Galileo felt extremely blessed to have made these amazing discoveries. But he would quickly find out that sometimes being chosen for great things means being unpopular.

Being Chosen Sometimes Means Being Unpopular:

This idea was very unpopular at the time and made many people mad. Believe it or not, the angriest people were the Church people! So why in the world would the Church be angry with Galileo's newfound discovery that the earth rotates around the sun? Because 1 Chronicles 16:30 (NIV) says, "The world is firmly established; it cannot be moved." The Church at that time believed the earth didn't move. They also believed that anyone who said the earth moved was against God and should be punished.

Galileo tried to explain that he wasn't calling the Scriptures a lie, he just believed they were being interpreted incorrectly. Even with his good heart and easygoing nature, Galileo was put in prison for a time. He was later sentenced to stay at his home under house arrest. House arrest means you are not allowed to leave your home…ever! Can you imagine having to stay inside every day for the rest of your life? And you think a few rainy days are bad!

The lawmakers at the time also ordered that all books he had written not be allowed to be sold or read. It took almost 100 years for this ban to be lifted. Good thing Galileo didn't wait for people to change their minds before writing his famous science books!

---

[6] "Galileo to Gamma Cephei," The Telescope: Contemporary Research, Timeless Technique, www.stardate.org http://telescopes.stardate.org/history/history. php#1608 (6/4/2012).

[7] "The Galileo Project, Satellites of Jupiter," http://galileo.rice.edu/sci/observations/jupiter_satellites.html (6/4/2012).

Chosen People Can't Be Stopped:

Sadly, Galileo had to finish out his life under house arrest. And, most people still thought he was ridiculous to believe that the earth rotated around the sun. But that didn't stop Galileo from his calling. He could have sat home pouting about how mistreated he had been, but Galileo did just the opposite. He wrote his finest scientific book ever. In fact, over 300 years later, one of the smartest men of all time, Albert Einstein, loved it. Galileo's work actually helped Albert Einstein develop his famous "Theory of Relativity."

Making History:

There is no doubt that Galileo Galilei made history. One of the biggest things done in his honor was the launching of the Galileo spacecraft, the first spaceship to fly around Jupiter[8]. He would have been so proud!

Outro:

Plenty of people have studied space throughout the years, but it's plain to see that Galileo did more than just study space. He chose to make some big discoveries that would rock his world and make lots of people mad. Chosen people don't care what they have to give up to follow the call and make history. That's why Galileo Galilei is today's Real Deal.

There are several variations for bringing this lesson alive for your children:

Variation No. 1:

For a dramatic impact, loosely memorize the "lines" of your lesson and deliver them in first person to your children. You'll captivate them and absolutely hook them on the science of today's lesson!

Variation No. 2:

For a science extension, study the stars and see what constellations you can find in the night sky. You can emphasize how even "the heavens declare the glory of God" (Psalm 19:1 KJV)!

Variation No. 3:

Watch a NOVA® video[9] on the orbit of the planets around the sun and discuss what novel ideas Galileo was introducing to the world in his support of Copernicanism.

Variation No. 4:

Make a planetary model out of polystyrene foam, clay or playdough for a three-dimensional look at the solar system. Manipulate your models so all the planets correctly revolve around the sun. Then, incorrectly arrange them, the way scientists in Galileo's time thought the solar system was organized. Kids will totally enjoy moving the universe!

---

[8] "Solar System Exploration: Galileo Legacy Site," National Aeronautics and Space Administration, http://solarsystem.nasa.gov/galileo (6/4/2012).

[9] Available free of charge online at http://video.pbs.org/program/nova.

DAY 5: GAME TIME — YOU CHOOSE!

Suggested Time: 10-15 minutes

Memory Verse: For God knew his people in advance, and he chose them to become like his Son, so that his Son would be the firstborn among many brothers and sisters.—Romans 8:29

Teacher Tip: Keep all miscellaneous items in a bag prior to playing, so that none of your kids can see what they are. Have small prizes for the winning team and their peers.

Supplies: ☐ Large bag or box, ☐ Blindfold, ☐ 12-20 Miscellaneous items, ☐ Table, ☐ Timer

Game Instructions:

Have one child put on a blindfold.

When you say, "go," the music and timer will start and the first contestant takes an item out and guesses what it is by feeling it. Remind players they only have one minute to guess as many as they can.

For each correct guess, the team or individual receives 1000 points. Wait until the time is up before revealing how many guesses are right.

Make sure the audience does not shout out the answers.

Game Goal:

The team or person with the highest correct total wins!

Final Word:

God, our Father, didn't guess what you were. He knows in advance how awesome you are. Not only that, He chose you—but He chose you to be just like Jesus. That makes us all winners!

Variation: Large Groups

For a larger group, divide players into two teams and use additional blindfolds and items. If you participate, you should have each person contribute items to the bag to be used in the game. They'll enjoy trying to "trick" you, too!

Notes: _____

_____

_____

_____

_____

ACTIVITY PAGE — SCRIPTURE MEMORY MATCH

Memory Verse: For God knew his people in advance, and he chose them to become like his Son, so that his Son would be the firstborn among many brothers and sisters. —Romans 8:29

Throughout the last several weeks, you've learned and studied many Bible verses about God's character in you. Today, you'll see just how well you remember the verses you've studied. Draw a line, matching the verse on the left with the correct reference on the right.

Scripture Memory Match

Children, obey your parents because you belong to the Lord, for this is the right thing to do. "Honor your father and mother." This is the first commandment with a promise.

Then God looked over all he had made, and he saw that it was very good!

I have revealed you to them, and I will continue to do so. Then your love for me will be in them, and I will be in them.

The thief's purpose is to steal and kill and destroy. My purpose is to give them a rich and satisfying life.

But I will honor those who honor me, and I will despise those who think lightly of me.

For even the Son of Man came not to be served but to serve others and to give his life as a ransom for many.

Trust in the Lord with all your heart; do not depend on your own understanding. Seek his will in all you do, and he will show you which path to take.

He sat down, called the twelve disciples over to him, and said, "Whoever wants to be first must take last place and be the servant of everyone else."

Honor your father and mother. Love your neighbor as yourself.

Everyone must submit to governing authorities. For all authority comes from God, and those in positions of authority have been placed there by God.

Ephesians 6:1-2

Romans 13:1

Matthew 20:28

Matthew 19:19

John 10:10

Mark 9:35

1 Samuel 2:30b

Proverbs 3:5-6

Genesis 1:31

John 17:26

ANSWER KEY

Children, obey your parents because you belong to the Lord, for this is the right thing to do. "Honor your father and mother." This is the first commandment with a promise.—Ephesians 6:1-2

Then God looked over all he had made, and he saw that it was very good!—Genesis 1:31

I have revealed you to them, and I will continue to do so. Then your love for me will be in them, and I will be in them. —John 17:26

The thief's purpose is to steal and kill and destroy. My purpose is to give them a rich and satisfying life.—John 10:10

But I will honor those who honor me, and I will despise those who think lightly of me.—1 Samuel 2:30b

For even the Son of Man came not to be served but to serve others and to give his life as a ransom for many.—Matthew 20:28

Trust in the Lord with all your heart; do not depend on your own understanding. Seek his will in all you do, and he will show you which path to take.—Proverbs 3:5-6

He sat down, called the twelve disciples over to him, and said, "Whoever wants to be first must take last place and be the servant of everyone else."—Mark 9:35

Honor your father and mother. Love your neighbor as yourself.—Matthew 19:19

Everyone must submit to governing authorities. For all authority comes from God, and those in positions of authority have been placed there by God.—Romans 13:1

Notes: _____

_____

_____

_____

_____

_____

_____

_____

_____

_____

_____

WEEK 12: YOU ARE RIGHTEOUS

Memory Verse: For He made Him who knew no sin to be sin for us, that we might become the righteousness of God in Him.—2 Corinthians 5:21 NKJV

WEEK 12: SNAPSHOT — YOU ARE RIGHTEOUS

DAY	TYPE OF LESSON	LESSON TITLE	SUPPLIES
Day 1	Bible Lesson	Righteous in Christ	None
Day 2	Object Lesson	No More Hiding	Table, Chair, Paper towels, Disinfectant spray, Trash can, Basket containing the following items: Tablecloth, Napkin, Water bottle, Any food item you can pretend not to like—just choose something the kids can relate to, Utensils (If you need them)
Day 3	Giving Lesson	Bursting With Goodness	Piñata filled with candy
Day 4	Academy Lab	Better Than New	Clear bowl (big enough to place your hand in), Clear pitcher with water, Iodine, Liquid starch, Vitamin C tablets crushed into powder, Large spoon, 1-Cup measure
Day 5	Game Time	Burst Your Bubble	Several packs of bubble gum (6 pieces needed per round of play), Bucket or container, Masking tape, Upbeat music
Bonus	Activity Page	Jesus and Nicodemus Coloring Page	1 Copy for each child

Lesson Introduction:

What a great day to awake to righteousness, and let it change us (1 Corinthians 15:34)!

Our righteousness in God is the greatest miracle He has ever offered us. When sin separated us from God, our spirits had no way to connect with Him. We were subject to anything Satan wanted to throw at us. There was nothing we could do to fix it.

Thank God He was unwilling to lose us!

As you teach this week, remember the whole picture of Romans 8. God *wanted* us! He paid the price for us! And now, all that He *has* and *is* belongs to us—not based on our own goodness, but on His.

Too many times we confuse righteousness with right conduct. Jesus' gift of righteousness causes us to *want* to act right. It isn't the other way around!

This is good news for us because nothing can come between us and God ever again. That thought is encapsulated in Romans 5:1-2. We have peace with God because of Jesus, and we can walk with Him in all His glory!

Love,

Commander Kellie

Commander Kellie

Lesson Outline:

As parents, we are constantly trying to teach our children to make good choices and to "be good." But, as we teach them about Jesus, let's be careful to teach them the good news that they *are* good enough because Jesus makes them righteous! It's not through effort or ability, but through the amazing power of God. What great news!

I. GOD PLANNED FOR US TO BE HIS FAMILY Romans 8:29-30

   a. Righteousness: The ability to stand before God without guilt or shame as if sin had never existed or separated us from God.

   b. Adam brought sin to all. Romans 5:12, 16

   c. Man's sin nature separated him from God. Ephesians 2:1-3

II. WE COULDN'T EARN RIGHTEOUSNESS, SO GOD GAVE US A GREAT GIFT Ephesians 2:4-6, 8-9

   a. God made Jesus to be our sin, so we could be made His righteousness! 2 Corinthians 5:21 NKJV

   b. Jesus made us right with God—as if we'd never sinned. Romans 5:10-11

   c. What Jesus did was more powerful than what Adam did! Romans 5:17-18

III. WE ARE MADE RIGHTEOUS BY BELIEVING AND SAYING WHAT GOD SAYS Romans 3:22-27

   a. No matter who we are or what we've done, He says we are righteous.

   b. Their righteousness is from Me, says the Lord. Isaiah 54:17 NKJV

   c. It's by faith from start to finish. Romans 1:17

   d. Believe in your heart, and say what God says! Romans 10:10

Notes: _____

_____

_____

_____

_____

_____

_____

_____

_____

_____

DAY 1: BIBLE LESSON — RIGHTEOUS IN CHRIST

Memory Verse: For He made Him who knew no sin to be sin for us, that we might become the righteousness of God in Him. —2 Corinthians 5:21 NKJV

Choosing to do the right thing is a part of life. Children are trained to behave acceptably and to receive consequences for unacceptable behavior. But, when it comes to eternal life, it's not based on performance. Acceptance by God, or being in right-standing with Him, is simply the gracious gift we receive when we believe in the Lord Jesus Christ. This week, take time to make sure children understand the basic truth of the gospel—that our good works do not redeem us—only Jesus does!

Read John 3:1-17:
Jesus Teaches Nicodemus

There was a man named Nicodemus, a Jewish religious leader who was a Pharisee. After dark one evening, he came to speak with Jesus. "Rabbi," he said, "we all know that God has sent you to teach us. Your miraculous signs are evidence that God is with you."

Jesus replied, "I tell you the truth, unless you are born again, you cannot see the Kingdom of God."

"What do you mean?" exclaimed Nicodemus. "How can an old man go back into his mother's womb and be born again?"

Jesus replied, "I assure you, no one can enter the Kingdom of God without being born of water and the Spirit. Humans can reproduce only human life, but the Holy Spirit gives birth to spiritual life. So don't be surprised when I say, 'You must be born again.' The wind blows wherever it wants. Just as you can hear the wind but can't tell where it comes from or where it is going, so you can't explain how people are born of the Spirit."

"How are these things possible?" Nicodemus asked.

Jesus replied, "You are a respected Jewish teacher, and yet you don't understand these things? I assure you, we tell you what we know and have seen, and yet you won't believe our testimony. But if you don't believe me when I tell you about earthly things, how can you possibly believe if I tell you about heavenly things? No one has ever gone to heaven and re-turned. But the Son of Man has come down from heaven. And as Moses lifted up the bronze snake on a pole in the wilderness, so the Son of Man must be lifted up, so that everyone who believes in him will have eternal life. For God loved the world so much that he gave his one and only Son, so that everyone who believes in him will not perish but have eternal life. God sent his Son into the world not to judge the world, but to save the world through him."

Discussion Questions:

1. What was the name of the man who approached Jesus late one night?
His name was Nicodemus. He was a Pharisee, a teacher of the Jewish law.

2. Why do you think he approached Jesus at night?
Answers will vary, but it's safe to assume he did not want to be seen.

3. What did Jesus tell Nicodemus he must do?
Jesus told him that he must be born again by the Spirit of God.

4. Nicodemus was a good man. Why wasn't that good enough for Jesus?

Our own righteousness—or trying to be good—cannot purchase our salvation. All the good things we do will not replace the fact that we must believe in our hearts and confess with our mouths that Jesus Christ is the Son of God, that He died on the cross for our sins and rose again the third day for us (Romans 10:9-10)!

5. What is the promise of believing in Jesus?

We will receive eternal life.

6. Why did God send Jesus?

He sent Jesus so that the world could be saved through His Son. Through Jesus, we are now in right-standing with God. We can now have a relationship with Him.

7. Do you think God wants us to feel bad that we can't be perfect?

No, God wants us to repent and confess our sin to Him when we do wrong, and then believe on Him to perfect us (1 John 1:9; Philippians 1:6). *He* makes us righteous or good!

8. The Pharisees were good people, always very careful about being good. But Jesus was always on their case. Why?

The Pharisees were good at "being good" on the outside and following rules, but Jesus wanted them to let God make their insides—their hearts—good, as well! We should not be "proud" of our own goodness, but remember that it is only God, through the sacrifice of His Son, Jesus, who has *made us His righteousness* (1 Corinthians 1:30)!

9. Does this mean we can do whatever we want and it doesn't matter because we've been made righteous through Jesus?

No, it doesn't mean that! We do what *He* wants us to do because we love Him so much and want to serve Him with all of our hearts. We follow His principles, and we know that Jesus is the "finisher" of our faith. So, He is perfecting us to be just like Him!

Notes: _____

_____

_____

_____

_____

_____

_____

_____

_____

_____

_____

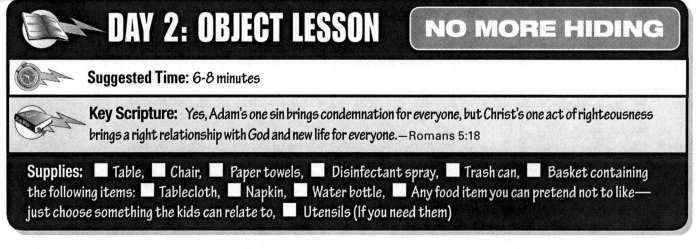

DAY 2: OBJECT LESSON — NO MORE HIDING

Suggested Time: *6-8 minutes*

Key Scripture: *Yes, Adam's one sin brings condemnation for everyone, but Christ's one act of righteousness brings a right relationship with God and new life for everyone.*—Romans 5:18

Supplies: ■ Table, ■ Chair, ■ Paper towels, ■ Disinfectant spray, ■ Trash can, ■ Basket containing the following items: ■ Tablecloth, ■ Napkin, ■ Water bottle, ■ Any food item you can pretend not to like— just choose something the kids can relate to, ■ Utensils (If you need them)

Lesson Instructions:

Grandma *(or Aunt _____ or someone believable to your children!)* is the greatest! She sent this amazing picnic basket surprise for me! *(Take tablecloth out of the basket and spread it over the table.)* Let's see…water to wash down my snack… *(Set the water bottle on the table.)* A napkin to wipe the delicious crumbs off my mouth…. *(Place the napkin nicely on the table.)* Annnnnd last, but certainly not least, drum roll please, the amazingly scrumptious, awesomely delectable, snack of yumminess…. It's _____*(Pull out your snack and look very disappointed as you announce what it is.).*

Bummer. I was hoping for some chocolate chip cookies or hot wings. I feel tempted not to eat it, but my mom *(or Aunt _____)* went to all this effort to put this basket together, I guess I'd better. Maybe it's better than it looks. *(Take a bite, then quickly make a face. This is your chance to be dramatic and make it funny.)* I'm not too sure about this. I know _____wants me to eat stuff like this sometimes, but I'm getting an idea. I've got it! I'll put it under this table-cloth. She'll never know, so her feelings won't be hurt. I'd better chew a few more bites to make it look like I liked it. *(Chew more bites, then spit each one out into your hand and put it under the tablecloth.)* I'm so glad she sent this tablecloth. It's great for hiding food.

Have any of you ever hidden chewed-up food before? Maybe you hid some in a napkin or pocket. What do you think would happen to this food if I left it under the tablecloth for a few weeks, or even a few months, or at least until _____ comes over to see if I enjoyed this basket?

(Get responses from your Superkids.)

It would start to STINK! It could even rot or gather bugs. The tablecloth may be able to hide it for a while, but eventually it would be discovered.

That is exactly like sin. When Adam disobeyed God in the Garden of Eden, he tried to hide it from God. It was no use, though—God could smell the STINK of sin and, sadly, it separated every person on the planet from Him. Romans 5:18 says Adam's one sin brought condemnation (dirtiness) for everyone, but Jesus' one act of righteousness brought a right relation-ship with God and new life for everyone. From our story this week, it looks like the real reason that Nicodemus went and talked to Jesus is that he was trying to be good and do everything he knew to be righteous, but he still felt dirty!

Our heavenly Father had a plan to fix everything! He sent Jesus. And Jesus knew just what to do to get rid of sin once and for all. *(Pull out your paper towels and cleaner.)* When Jesus died on the cross, He took our sin and made us right with God! *(Take the items off the table and then remove the dirty tablecloth.)* He wiped us completely clean from sin—that's what being "righteous" means. *(Wipe off your table with the paper towels and cleaner.)* Because of Jesus, it's like we have never done a wrong thing in our entire lives! *(Throw paper towels into the trash can.)*

Just think how great that is! Now, you don't have to be like this tablecloth—hiding nasty, rotten, chewed-up sin. With Jesus, your life can be clean and righteous so you never stink on the inside! And when our lives smell good, we can stand boldly before God.

Good thing I had some paper towels and cleaner here. Now this table is "righteous" too!

Notes: _____

_____

_____

_____

_____

_____

_____

_____

_____

_____

_____

_____

_____

_____

_____

_____

_____

_____

_____

_____

_____

_____

_____

_____

_____

DAY 3: GIVING LESSON

BURSTING WITH GOODNESS

Suggested Time: 10 minutes

Offering Scripture: Your generosity will surprise him (your enemy) with goodness. —Romans 12:20 MSG

Supplies: ☐ Piñata filled with candy

Lesson Instructions:

Have you ever been to a party where they had one of these? *(Show your piñata.)* Can anyone tell me how they work? What was your experience like? *(Offer time to share).*

Let me ask you a question: Piñatas are filled with something good, but do we know exactly what is in there? No, we don't know what kind of goodies are on the inside until they all come spilling out. It's a surprise!

Today, I want to tell you about a surprise pouring out of a different kind of "piñata" that God thinks is pretty special. In Romans 12:20 it says, "Your generosity will surprise him with goodness." This verse tells us that when we are generous to others it will be like a nice surprise to those we are giving to.

Picture it like this: When you are full of generosity and give kindness, your heart is like this piñata, full of goodness. And when you begin giving to others it's like a piñata breaking open and awesome surprises falling out to those around you.

How pleased our heavenly Father must be when you have a generous heart and let that goodness spill out to others, showering them with sweet surprises. In fact, why don't you bring some sweet surprises to God today as you prepare to give this week's tithes and offerings to Him?

Variation: Shower With Blessing

Choose someone in your church family, community or neighborhood whom you would like to "shower" with a blessing. Prepare a gift basket, write notes and drop it by. If it's an elderly person, they would probably love the visit. Have your kids brainstorm what type of goodies should go inside. You'll be amazed at their ingenuity and sincerity in giving. Let their generosity overflow and be a blessing to someone you know.

Notes: _____

_____

_____

_____

_____

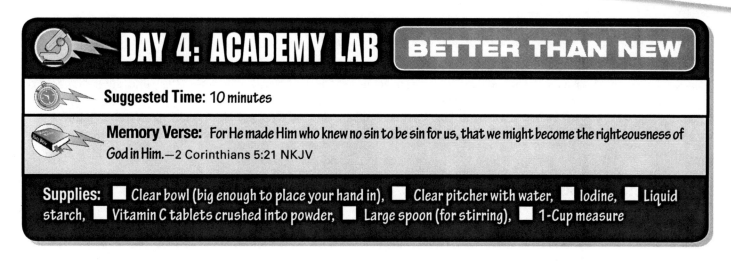

DAY 4: ACADEMY LAB BETTER THAN NEW

Suggested Time: 10 minutes

Memory Verse: For He made Him who knew no sin to be sin for us, that we might become the righteousness of God in Him.—2 Corinthians 5:21 NKJV

Supplies: ☐ Clear bowl (big enough to place your hand in), ☐ Clear pitcher with water, ☐ Iodine, ☐ Liquid starch, ☐ Vitamin C tablets crushed into powder, ☐ Large spoon (for stirring), ☐ 1-Cup measure

Experiment:

1. Pour one cup of liquid starch into the bowl.

2. Put several drops of iodine into the pitcher and stir until the water turns light yellow.

3. Put your right hand in the water and stir it around.

4. Put your left hand into the bowl with the starch, so that your hand is covered.

5. Take your right hand out of the pitcher and place your left hand (that's covered with starch) into the pitcher and swish it around. The water will turn blue.

6. Remove your left hand from the water. Have one of the kids dump the vitamin C powder (it may take two or more tablets to make a dramatic change) into your right hand.

7. Place your right hand into the water and swish it around as you release the powder. You should see the water turn clear again.

Lesson Instructions:

In our experiment today, I want to show you how to transform this pitcher of water. As good scientists, you'll want to make astute observations about what is taking place and why.

Let's begin with a pitcher of clear water. This clean water is exactly how God made man in the beginning—absolutely perfect and pure. But I think most of you know what happened to those two clean and pure people when the devil showed up. They listened to a lie and disobeyed God, introducing sin into the world. It's kind of like what happens to this water when I add a little iodine. What are your observations? What happened?

The water now looks like Adam and Eve's hearts after they sinned in the garden, their hearts were no longer clean and pure.

Boys and girls, there was only one way for this dirty heart problem to be solved. Before things got fixed between God and His kids, the situation actually got worse. Let me show you what I mean. *(Do steps 4 and 5 to turn the water blue.)*

Can you see how this water has gotten even darker than before? Jesus took all the dirtiness of sin, like this dirty water, on Himself when He went to the cross. That was a dark day for God and His only Son!

But I'm so glad the story doesn't end there. After Jesus paid for our sins, something awesome happened! *(Complete the experiment by following steps 6 and 7.)*

How cool! The water isn't dark and dirty anymore. Because Jesus took the blame for the sins of the world, our hearts aren't dirty anymore, either. In fact, this is just like when Jesus told Nicodemus that he "must be born again." When we accept what He did for us by becoming "born again," our hearts become clean and clear just like this pitcher of water. And with clean hearts, we have the privilege of being close to God all the time—and that's something to get excited about, wouldn't you agree?

Variation: Science Journal

Have students record their observations in a science journal. For the young student, draw a picture of what they see each time, adding labels that will show what is drawn in the pitcher. For older students, discuss the reason behind the color changes. What chemicals are reacting and emitting color into the water?

Notes: _____

_____

_____

_____

_____

_____

_____

_____

_____

_____

_____

_____

_____

_____

_____

_____

_____

_____

_____

_____

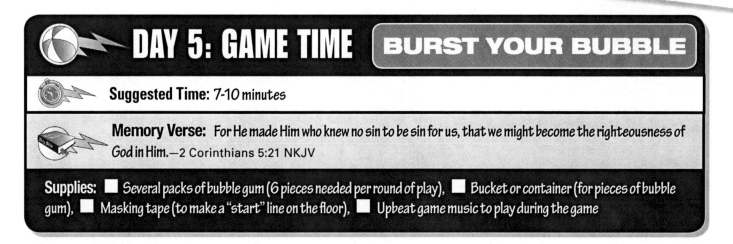

DAY 5: GAME TIME — **BURST YOUR BUBBLE**

Suggested Time: 7-10 minutes

Memory Verse: For He made Him who knew no sin to be sin for us, that we might become the righteousness of God in Him.—2 Corinthians 5:21 NKJV

Supplies: ■ Several packs of bubble gum (6 pieces needed per round of play), ■ Bucket or container (for pieces of bubble gum), ■ Masking tape (to make a "start" line on the floor), ■ Upbeat game music to play during the game

Prior to Game:

- Open packs of bubble gum and put individually wrapped pieces into your bucket or container.

- Place the bucket of bubble gum at the front of room. Use masking tape to make a "start" line on your floor a good distance away from the bucket of bubble gum.

Game Instructions:

- Teach the memory verse to your kids, then divide into two teams.

- Have each team line up behind the "start" line.

- On "Go!" the first player on each team will say the memory verse as quickly as possible. Once they have completed it, they will run and retrieve a piece of gum from the bucket, open it up, chew it and blow a bubble.

- The player then returns to the front of the room to tag the next one in line.

Game Goal:

Learn God's Word well enough that it comes out quickly!

Final Word:

When we have Jesus living on the inside of us, we get to live in His righteousness. It's like living in a big God "bubble"!

Variation No. 1: Bubbles

Younger kids will not enjoy racing to create bubbles with bubble gum, so try having soapy bubbles for blowing. Each team will have a container of bubble-blowing liquid and can race back, blowing as many bubbles as possible.

Variation No. 2: Bubble Machine

If your kids aren't very competitive or you need to change up the flavor of your memory verse time, eliminate the competition altogether by turning on a bubble machine with fun colored bubbles and saying the memory verse together. You could say it in elephant (loud) voices, mouse (squeaky) voices, spider (whisper) voices, or any variation you might prefer. It's sure to be fun, and God's Word will be hidden in their hearts!

Notes: _____

_____

_____

_____

_____

_____

_____

_____

_____

_____

_____

_____

_____

_____

_____

_____

_____

_____

_____

_____

_____

_____

_____

_____

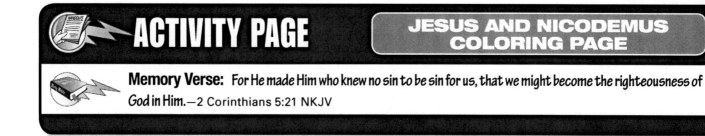

ACTIVITY PAGE

JESUS AND NICODEMUS COLORING PAGE

Memory Verse: For He made Him who knew no sin to be sin for us, that we might become the righteousness of God in Him.—2 Corinthians 5:21 NKJV

This week, you read about Jesus' conversation with Nicodemus in John 3:1-17. Now, have fun coloring this scene of that important conversation.

Notes: _____

_____

_____

_____

_____

_____

_____

_____

_____

_____

_____

_____

_____

_____

_____

_____

_____

_____

_____

_____

_____

_____

_____

_____

_____

_____

_____

_____

_____

_____

_____

_____

_____

_____

WEEK 13: YOU ARE BLESSED

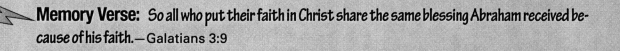

Memory Verse: *So all who put their faith in Christ share the same blessing Abraham received because of his faith.*—Galatians 3:9

WEEK 13: SNAPSHOT — YOU ARE BLESSED

DAY	TYPE OF LESSON	LESSON TITLE	SUPPLIES
Day 1	Bible Lesson	Whom Will You Choose?	None
Day 2	Storybook Theater	Emerald	Whiteboard or chalkboard or easel with paper, Markers or pastel chalks, Rags (to blend chalks), Pencil and eraser (art pencils work best), Art smock, **Optional costumes:** Red wig, Brightly colored "girly" T-shirt (for Em), Blond or brown wig, T-shirt (for classmate), "Mom"-type wig, Blouse and necklace (for Mom), Leather jacket, Crazy wig and beard, Bandana (for Pastor Rod)
Day 3	Giving Lesson	God's Benefits	Classified section of newspapers (employment section)
Day 4	Object Lesson	An Easy Choice	Chocolate cream pie, Premade pie shell, Pie server, Whipped cream in a can, Soil, Water, Fork, Pie server utensil, Table, Plastic tablecloth, Regular tablecloth or sheet
Day 5	Game Time	Let's Eat	8 Pudding or gelatin dessert cups, 8 Spoons, Plastic tarp
Bonus	Activity Page	We Are Blessed Double Puzzle	1 Copy for each child

Lesson Introduction:

This week's lesson includes way too much Scripture to teach it all in a mere five days. That's because these scriptures are for you, the teacher! Take some extra prayer and study time this week to really let the Word of God sink in! Allow the Lord to let the revelation of THE BLESSING explode in you! There is no greater life than to walk in THE BLESSING of God here on earth.

Numerous times, we have taught our Superkids about "The Sweet Life." Life with God is not about following a list of dos and don'ts—it is about living in THE BLESSING! It's about not experimenting with our own choices. God has already laid out a plan for our lives and blessed it! We just need to listen and obey.

We don't even need all the details when we put our confidence in Him (Proverbs 20:24). Deuteronomy 30:11 tells us it isn't hard or complicated. Just choose His way!

Just like Jesus, we can be right every time. Jesus didn't find His perfection in being the Son of God—He found it in being obedient.

Read John 5:30 in *The Amplified Bible.* As He is, so are we! Obedient and BLESSED! Then, reflect on Romans 8. He makes things work for us (verse 28), He's given us His glory (verse 30) and everything else (verse 32)! He is for us—who can be against us? That's THE BLESSING! Just live it!

Love,

Commander Kellie

Commander Kellie

Lesson Outline:

The most powerful testimony your children will ever see or hear is yours! This week, be determined to walk in THE BLESSING of God and watch Him open doors for you to minister to your children. He has promised blessings to you!

I. GOD CALLED HIS PEOPLE TO WALK IN THE BLESSING Romans 8:30-39

   a. Adam and Eve chose their own way. Genesis 1:28-29, 2:8-9, 3:17-19

   b. Noah's family wanted to be famous without God. Genesis 9:1-3, 11:3-4

   c. Abraham let God make him rich and famous—that's THE BLESSING. Genesis 12:1-3, 14:17-23

   d. Circumstances couldn't keep Isaac, Jacob or Joseph down either. They all walked in THE BLESSING!

II. JESUS PURCHASED THE BLESSING FOR US Galatians 3:13-14 NKJV

   a. God must be our source—have faith in Him. Matthew 6:24-33

   b. When we do things God's way, we are BLESSED. 2 Peter 1:3-11

   c. THE BLESSING makes you truly rich, without sorrow and toiling. Proverbs 10:22 AMP

III. WE MUST CHOOSE THE BLESSING OR THE CURSE Deuteronomy 30:15-20

   a. Obedience is the key to THE BLESSING. Deuteronomy 28:1-2, 8, 13

   b. Even for kids! Ephesians 6:1-3

   c. It is your choice.

   d. "The Sweet Life." Ephesians 2:10 AMP

   e. The Swampy Life. Proverbs 13:15 AMP

Notes: _____

_____

_____

_____

_____

_____

DAY 1: BIBLE LESSON — WHOM WILL YOU CHOOSE?

Memory Verse: *So all who put their faith in Christ share the same blessing Abraham received because of his faith.*—Galatians 3:9

As believers, it is easy for us to assume that our kids are "choosing" to follow God, but sometimes we can get caught up in presenting to them a cultural version of Him. Without even realizing it, we can portray Him as just another element in our Christian lives along with church, Scripture memory and being good. Let the Lord work through you this week as you share with your kids and make sure that they are making the *choice* to follow Him and walk in THE BLESSING that He has promised to those who obey and trust in Him!

Read Joshua 24:2-15:
To the People

Joshua said to the people, "This is what the Lord, the God of Israel, says: Long ago your ancestors, including Terah, the father of Abraham and Nahor, lived beyond the Euphrates River, and they worshiped other gods. But I took your ancestor Abraham from the land beyond the Euphrates and led him into the land of Canaan. I gave him many descendants through his son Isaac. To Isaac I gave Jacob and Esau. To Esau I gave the mountains of Seir, while Jacob and his children went down into Egypt.

"Then I sent Moses and Aaron, and I brought terrible plagues on Egypt; and afterward I brought you out as a free people. But when your ancestors arrived at the Red Sea, the Egyptians chased after you with chariots and charioteers. When your ancestors cried out to the Lord, I put darkness between you and the Egyptians. I brought the sea crashing down on the Egyptians, drowning them. With your very own eyes you saw what I did. Then you lived in the wilderness for many years.

"Finally, I brought you into the land of the Amorites on the east side of the Jordan. They fought against you, but I destroyed them before you. I gave you victory over them, and you took possession of their land. Then Balak son of Zippor, king of Moab, started a war against Israel. He summoned Balaam son of Beor to curse you, but I would not listen to him. Instead, I made Balaam bless you, and so I rescued you from Balak.

"When you crossed the Jordan River and came to Jericho, the men of Jericho fought against you, as did the Amorites, the Perizzites, the Canaanites, the Hittites, the Girgashites, the Hivites, and the Jebusites. But I gave you victory over them. And I sent terror ahead of you to drive out the two kings of the Amorites. It was not your swords or bows that brought you victory. I gave you land you had not worked on, and I gave you towns you did not build—the towns where you are now living. I gave you vineyards and olive groves for food, though you did not plant them.

"So fear the Lord and serve him wholeheartedly. Put away forever the idols your ancestors worshiped when they lived beyond the Euphrates River and in Egypt. Serve the Lord alone. But if you refuse to serve the Lord, then choose today whom you will serve. Would you prefer the gods your ancestors served beyond the Euphrates? Or will it be the gods of the Amorites in whose land you now live? But as for me and my family, we will serve the Lord."

Discussion Questions

1. Joshua is preaching this long sermon, but of what is he reminding the people of Israel?
  That they have a history of God rescuing and blessing them!

2. Name some of the people Joshua mentions.
He mentions Abraham, Isaac, Esau, Jacob, the Israelites in Egypt, Moses, Aaron and Balaam.

3. What is Joshua's message?
Answers will vary, but they should include the point that Joshua wants the people to choose to serve the Lord.

4. What does Joshua decide?
He says that "as for me and my house, we will serve the Lord."

5. At that moment, they were in the Promised Land receiving their inheritance. Why is that significant?
God always gives a choice whether or not we will follow Him and receive His blessings.

6. What are some of God's promises to you?
Answers will vary.

Variation: Map Skills

Find the cities, lands and bodies of water listed in this passage on a Bible map or a world map. You could even print out a map from the Internet, and allow your children to mark and label the landmarks.

Notes: _____

_____

_____

_____

_____

_____

_____

_____

_____

_____

_____

_____

_____

_____

_____

_____

_____

_____

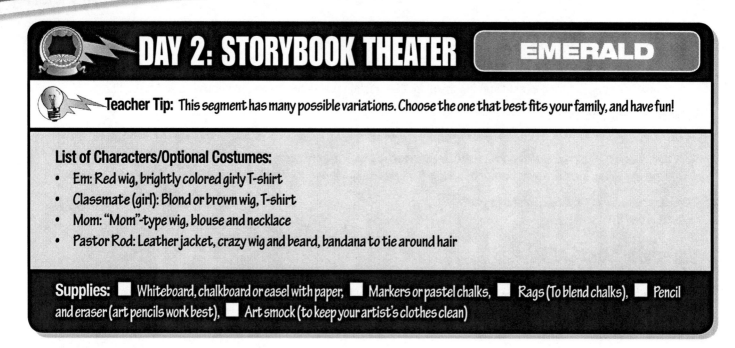

DAY 2: STORYBOOK THEATER — EMERALD

Teacher Tip: This segment has many possible variations. Choose the one that best fits your family, and have fun!

List of Characters/Optional Costumes:

- Em: Red wig, brightly colored girly T-shirt
- Classmate (girl): Blond or brown wig, T-shirt
- Mom: "Mom"-type wig, blouse and necklace
- Pastor Rod: Leather jacket, crazy wig and beard, bandana to tie around hair

Supplies: ☐ Whiteboard, chalkboard or easel with paper, ☐ Markers or pastel chalks, ☐ Rags (To blend chalks), ☐ Pencil and eraser (art pencils work best), ☐ Art smock (to keep your artist's clothes clean)

Variation No. 1:

Read the story as part of your read-aloud time.

Variation No. 2:

Read the story like an old-time radio skit, complete with different actors for each part. If you are limited on participants, then allow more than one part per person and change the voice. Make copies of the skit, and have each actor highlight their lines.

Variation No. 3:

Act out the story as a fun skit. Perhaps your children can practice during the day (even creating fun costumes from everyday items) and then perform it in the evening for the whole family. Before beginning your skit, remember to introduce your cast!

Variation No. 4:

Create a storybook theater where one or more family members sketch the story on a whiteboard, chalkboard or artist's easel, as another member reads the story. Initially, there will be a few supplies to purchase, but don't let this be a deterrent from using the illustrated story option! Once the supplies have been purchased, they'll be long-lasting and reusable. Teacher tip: Cut the paper to fit on the board and tape it down. Lightly sketch the drawing with a pencil prior to presentation. Time may not allow for the picture to be completely drawn and colored during the story. Erase the pencil lines, so light lines are visible to you but not to your audience. Review the story ahead of time to determine the amount of time needed to complete the illustration while telling the story. When the story begins, use black markers to draw the picture, tracing your pencil lines. Next, apply color using the pastel chalk. Then, blend the color with the rags to complete the picture.

Story:

Em was in fourth grade, and she wasn't happy about it. In fact, Em wasn't happy about a lot of things, and the worst one of all was her green eyes. The youngest of four girls, Em was the only one who looked, well, different. Her older sisters all had their mother's blue eyes and brown hair. But, not Em. No, she had very fair skin, reddish-blond hair and the greenest eyes in her class—the *only* green eyes in her class, actually. Last week in science class, her teacher had conducted an eye-color test, with everyone having brown eyes in one group, kids with blue eyes in another group, and there was Em, the only green-eyed girl in fourth grade. She felt out of place and sort of stupid, like there was something wrong with her.

Why me? she thought to herself as the teacher droned on about something called genetics.

Why can't I just look like everyone else instead of having these ugly green eyes?

And, why did her parents have to name her "Emerald," after those awful eyes? That made it even harder to forget how different she was.

Finally, class was over, and everyone grabbed their lunches. Em walked over to sit with some of the other girls and put her lunchbox on the table.

"Excuse me, this table is for blue eyes only—no emerald eyes here!"

It was the most embarrassing thing! Em wished she could be invisible. Thank the Lord it was Friday! Maybe by the time school started on Monday, everyone would have forgotten about eye color and genetics.

When she got home, she saw the coolest-looking motorcycle in the driveway. There was an eagle painted on it with the words, "You Can't Ride a Harley in Hell."

I wonder what that's about? she thought, opening the front door.

Em heard voices in the kitchen and went to investigate. Sitting at the kitchen table with her parents was a large man she had never seen before.

"Oh, hi, honey," her mom said. "This is Pastor Rod, and he's going to be speaking at church on Sunday."

"Hello," Em said quietly, staring at the floor.

Pastor Rod looked big sitting on the small kitchen chair, but when he stood up to meet her he was enormous!

With a voice to match his frame, he spoke with a rough, deep growl, "Hi there, little lady, how was your day? I'm Pastor Rod."

As Em looked up, she saw a very friendly face that was covered with long and somewhat wild hair.

"It wwwwas OK, I guess," replied Em, stuttering a bit. "Where do you get your hair cut?"

Em's mom immediately gave her one of "those" looks, but the big man threw back his head and laughed out loud.

"That's a great question!" he exclaimed, the smile even bigger than before. "Pretty much nowhere."

Her dad chuckled and Em breathed a sigh of relief. Maybe she wouldn't get a lecture later about proper conversation. Mom spoke up. "Go wash up honey, dinner's on."

As Em washed her hands, she couldn't help but like this unusual pastor, and wondered what he would preach about on Sunday. During dinner, Pastor Rod told some of the most interesting stories about what he called his "biker days." Apparently, he had ridden motorcycles all of his life and had lots of adventures. Some of them sounded scary to Em, but she tried not to ask too many questions. It seemed like most of Pastor Rod's stories ended with someone giving their heart to the Lord. By the time bedtime had rolled around, Em had forgotten all about green eyes and the fourth grade.

Before she knew it, Sunday was here. When Em's family got to church, they sat in the third row, as usual. When Pastor Rod was introduced, Em sat up and leaned forward. *I wonder if he will tell some more biker stories,* she thought to herself. Her new friend smiled at the congregation and told a story Em had not heard about yet.

"When I was a young man, I did not know Jesus. I didn't know He loved me, and that He gave His clean and perfect life for my dirty and ruined one. I was one of those rebellious bikers some of you may have heard about on the news from time to time. I hated anyone who was different from me, and I caused a lot of people to suffer." Pastor Rod paused, "Then one night, as I was sleeping, something happened that changed everything."

Em scooted to the edge of her seat as Pastor Rod continued.

"I dreamed that I was standing in front of a beautiful throne. Someone was sitting on the throne, and even though I couldn't see Him very clearly, I knew it was Jesus. He told me that I was lost and He wanted me to be found."

Pastor Rod looked around the room.

"You see, people, even though no one had ever introduced me to Jesus, I knew it was Him. That's the way He is—when you meet Him, you know it. I found my Savior that day, and decided I was going to find guys who were lost like I used to be and introduce them to Jesus, because He can take something we think is ugly and make something beautiful out of it."

The room was quiet. Pastor Rod opened a large, black Bible and began to read:

"I saw a throne and someone sitting on it. The one sitting on the throne was as brilliant as gemstones—like jasper and carnelian.

"And the glow of emerald circled His throne like a rainbow."

Pastor Rod looked up and closed his Bible.

"Em, would you come up here with me?" he asked.

Em wondered if her ears were playing tricks on her. The big man walked down from the pulpit and reached for her hand. Em stood up and let him lead her to the front.

"I saw that rainbow," Pastor Rod said softly. "It was as green as this girl's beautiful, emerald eyes." Looking down at her, Pastor Rod continued.

"Em, the other night when I first saw your eyes I thought of the day I made Jesus my Lord. Green became my favorite color that day! From this day forward, every time you look in a mirror, I want you to remember that God made a rainbow the color of emerald over the throne of His Son."

Riding home from church, Em felt completely different about having green eyes. In fact, she felt blessed that she had emerald eyes! Em's mom looked at her youngest daughter in the back seat and smiled.

Story by Dana Johnson

Notes:_____

_____

_____

_____

_____